MISSIONARY

ST PAUL'S OR OURS?

By the same author

*The Spontaneous Expansion of the Church:
and the Causes which Hinder it*

companion volume to

Missionary Methods

The Ministry of the Spirit
Selected writings of Roland Allen
With a Memoir by Alexander McLeish
Edited by David Paton

MISSIONARY METHODS

ST PAUL'S OR OURS?

BY

ROLAND ALLEN

Wm. B. Eerdmans Publishing Co.
Grand Rapids, Michigan

American Edition 1962
© Copyright 1962, World Dominion Press
All rights reserved
Printed in the United States of America

Foreword © Copyright
Wm. B. Eerdmans Publishing Co. 1962

10 09 08 07 06 05 04   29 28 27 26 25 24 23

ISBN 0-8028-1001-2

PHOTOLITHOPRINTED BY EERDMANS PRINTING COMPANY
GRAND RAPIDS, MICHIGAN, UNITED STATES OF AMERICA

Foreword

It is an unusual privilege to be asked to write the introduction to a book published 40 years ago and now in its sixth edition. But this is an unusual book. I vividly remember my first reading of it. Roland Allen has a style of writing which can be almost infuriating. He takes hold of you and refuses to let you go till you have admitted that he is right. Whichever way you turn, he has an argument to silence you. The reader should be warned that this is a book which compels decisions!

Roland Allen was an Anglican missionary in China from 1895 to 1903. For a few years afterward he was in charge of an English parish. For the next 40 years he was writing on missionary principles. Much of what he wrote seemed to be forgotten. The present work and a later volume written in answer to criticisms (*The Spontaneous Expansion of the Church and the Causes which Hinder It*) are the only two that have been regularly reprinted. Allen himself told his son that his writings would come into their own about the year 1960. In fact that year saw the republication in a single volume of many of his other writings (*The Ministry of the Spirit*). But his voice has not been silent during these 40 years. Quietly but insistently it has continued to challenge the accepted assumptions of churches and missions, and slowly but steadily the number of those who found themselves compelled to listen has increased.

Perhaps one word in the title of the present work is unfortunate — the word 'Methods'. If anyone thinks that he will find here a 'method' which can forthwith be 'applied', he is in for trouble. Allen's own understanding of what he was doing is well conveyed by the following words written in 1932 after visiting mission work in East Africa: "I never ask anyone to *do* anything and consequently I do not get a 'yes' or 'no.' I say what seems to me obviously true, but they do not know what to do about it. One day someone will see what action is demanded, and perhaps screw up their courage to take it. If I were out to organize and lead, that would

i

be different, but as you well know I long ago determined that that was not the way of the Spirit for me. . . . All I can say is 'This is the way of Christ and His Apostles'. If any man answers, 'That is out of date', or 'Times have changed'. . . I can only repeat 'This is the way of Christ and His Apostles', and leave him to face that issue."

Allen has been doing that, quietly but insistently, for these 40 years. I have been compelled, reluctantly, to face his question, and I have watched others being likewise compelled. But it can only be what Allen intended if it is the compulsion of the Spirit. The very heart and life of his message was that the mission of the Church is the work of the Spirit. I have known in my own experience the long years of wrestling with these issues which were needed before a Church was willing to put some of Allen's ideas to the test. But those years of wrestling were not mere 'preliminaries'; they were not an unfortunate necessity arising from the slowness and dullness of committees and clerics. They were part of the essential thing that Allen was concerned about — the resubmission in each generation of the traditions of men to the Word and Spirit of God. On the other hand, I have heard of mission boards which decided to 'apply' Allen's methods, and proceeded to issue instructions to 'the field' accordingly. The result could only be disaster. There are no 'methods' here which will 'work' if they are 'applied'. There is a summons to everyone who will hear to submit inherited patterns of Church life to the searching scrutiny of the Spirit.

I think that another word of caution is also in order. Allen was a missionary of the Society for the Propagation of the Gospel. He was a priest of the Church of England nurtured in the Catholic understanding of churchmanship. He was a High Churchman. His ideas about the centrality of the Spirit in missions brought him into fellowship with men of very different kinds of churchmanship. One of them has written of their work together as follows: "Allen's ecclesiastical outlook hardly came into our discussions. We were not interested in the ministry and the sacraments in the way that he was; he joined us in a deep concern for the place and pre-eminence of the Holy Spirit in all the work of the Church everywhere, and in the practical activities that this conviction involved." These words illuminate much of what has happened to Allen's message in these 40 years. Of too many of his interpreters it must be said that they were "not interested in the ministry and the sacraments in the way that he was." In Allen's thought — so far as I understand it — the central place given to the work of the Spirit in no way implied a lessening of the importance of the ordered life of the Church as one divine society bound together in a single visible fellowship with the Lord and His apostles, and visibly united in the sacramental life. If he does not speak much of this, it is because he takes it for granted and seeks to gain a hearing for the aspects of the Spirit's work which have been too much neglected in the tradition in which he was nurtured. To forget this and to read what he says about the work of the Spirit through the spectacles of a tradition which gives little place to order, ministry, and sacrament, can only lead to an atomising of the Church, which Allen would certainly have repudiated.

I have thought it right to enter these two words of caution, because the reader should be warned that he is embarking on a serious undertaking. Once he has started reading Allen, he will be compelled to go on. He will find that this quiet voice has a strange relevance and immediacy to the problems of the Church in our day. And I shall be surprised if he does not find before long that many of his accustomed ideas are being questioned by a voice more searching than the word of man.

—LESSLIE NEWBIGIN (BISHOP)

Publisher's Foreword

Roland Allen was a missionary in North China working with the Society for the Propagation of the Gospel. Later, he worked for a number of years in collaboration with the founders of *World Dominion* and the Survey Application Trust, and finally retired to Africa, where he died in Kenya in 1947.

The demand for his books still continues and makes it necessary to issue a new edition of *Missionary Methods*.

When Allen's careful analysis first appeared forty-eight years ago it made a startling impression. Many thoughtful missionaries and mission-secretaries throughout the world were forced to look at their own work afresh and ask themselves several awkward questions, such as: Is our progress commensurate with all the money and effort expended? Is that progress, if any, as rapid as the work of church-planting by the great Apostle? Are we actually planting new churches or merely perpetuating a mission? Are the new causes truly indigenous and self-supporting, and, if not, why not? At what stage in church-building does a missionary become dispensable?

The book divides into five parts. The first consists of a careful examination of how the Apostle came to visit the various centres and what conditions were like in the social and religious world of about AD 50. It is obvious that the author studied those conditions with great care and he quotes where necessary from the works of dependable authorities. The conclusion is that St Paul enjoyed no peculiar advantages in proclaiming the Gospel.

The second part comes to grips with the main problem by showing how St Paul presented the Christian Gospel, the significance of the miracles he performed, his financial policy of self-support for himself and self-support for the new churches, too, and how missionary methods of the nineteenth and twentieth centuries contrast with his alarmingly.

Part three stresses the short time devoted by St Paul to training converts before they were baptized, and the contrast between the rapid manner of appointing responsible church leaders in his day with the slowness of the present, together with our unconscious 'suppression' and 'silencing' of natural leaders and prophets.

This part of the book naturally disturbs missionary readers and provokes thought.

Part four deals with problems of authority and discipline in the churches, contrasting the Apostle's principles and actions with modern procedures which have failed to challenge the conscience of the local church. After all, it is what his own church thinks that ultimately influences an offender to mend his ways. This part ends with a stirring chapter on building the unity of the Church by spiritual means and by Christian fellowship rather than by the importation of Western systems artificially imposed upon the young Church.

Part five deals with conclusions. Roland Allen writes with such clarity and with such emphasis upon the Apostle's successful principles that the interest of the reader in the main theme is sustained to the end.

In recent years there has been a renewed interest in this book and in other writings of Allen. No doubt this is due to the fact that, in many parts of the world, churches and missions are being forced by circumstances to face the arguments which Allen so ably deployed nearly half-a-century ago. He himself used to say that fifty years would pass before his views would win wide assent and influence policy and practice.

The modern reader may well find his style repetitive, and sometimes even tedious. But who can blame Allen? In spite of many previous editions, it is still only the few who have heeded his teaching. It is in order that this book may continue to be studied, and may attract many new readers, that the World Dominion Press has republished it in its present form.

KENNETH G. GRUBB

December, 1960

Author's Preface

It is now fifteen years since this book was first published, and it is thought that a new and cheaper edition may be useful. In these fifteen years I have seen, and I have heard from others, that action in many parts of the world has been influenced by the study of St Paul's missionary methods; and I myself am more convinced than ever that in the careful examination of his work, above all in the understanding and appreciation of his *principles*, we shall find the solution of most of our present difficulties. We are talking today of indigenous churches. St Paul's churches were indigenous churches in the proper sense of the word; and I believe that the secret of their foundation lay in his recognition of the church as a local church (as opposed to our 'national churches') and in his profound belief and trust in the Holy Spirit indwelling his converts and the churches of which they were members, which enabled him to establish them at once with full authority. It is not easy for us today so to trust the Holy Ghost. We can more easily believe in His work in us and through us, than we can believe in His work in and through our converts: we cannot trust our converts to Him. But that is one of the most obvious lessons which the study of St Paul's work teaches us. I believe that we have still much to learn from his example.

In the reviews which appeared when this book was first published I was surprised and pleased to find that little fault was found with my statement of the Apostolic practice. Accepting the statement of the facts as substantially true, critics almost invariably fixed on two points: (1) that the gulf between us and the people to whom we go is deeper and wider than that between St Paul and those to whom he preached; (2) that he could rely upon converts from the synagogue to preserve his churches from dangers only too plain to us. The conclusion drawn was that what was possible for him in his day is impossible for us in ours.

To the first of these criticisms I replied in a book entitled *Educa-*

tional Principles and Missionary Methods,[1] in which I argued that the greater the gulf the greater was the value of the apostolic method. That argument is too long to summarize here. To the second I may say here briefly: (1) That the dangers which we anticipate, the dangers of lowering a standard of morals, or of a confusion of Christian doctrine by the introduction of ideas borrowed from heathen philosophy or superstition, were not less in his day than in ours; (2) that the breach between the Synagogue and the Christian Church arose so early and was so wide that as a matter of fact churches were soon being established which certainly were not 'off-shoots of the local synagogue', and yet the apostolic practice was maintained; (3) that at Corinth, and in Galatia, and in Ephesus, the presence of Jews or proselytes in the church did not prevent the dangers from arising; if St Paul relied upon them, they failed him; (4) that the argument demands that we should admit that Mosaic teaching is a better foundation for Christian morality and theology than the teaching of Christ and of the Holy Spirit; (5) that St Paul's faith in Christ and in His Holy Spirit would have forced him to act as he did, under any circumstances. He could not have relied upon any power either in heathen philosophic, or in Mosaic, teaching to establish his converts, under any circumstances whatsoever; (6) that if we went to China or to India and told those people that in morality and intelligence they were so far beneath the provincial Jews and proselytes of St Paul's day that he could not have dealt with them as he did with the provincials of Galatia, they would be insulted, and we should be saying what we should find it hard to prove. And if anyone answers me that when we use such speech we are thinking only of people in Africa and other uncivilized lands, I must reply that we are plainly thinking of all men everywhere, because we everywhere employ the same method, and everywhere alike shrink from establishing the Church on the apostolic plan.

In the light of experience gained in the last fifteen years I might have enlarged this book, but it did not seem wise to add greatly to its bulk. I have therefore contented myself with making as few corrections and additions as possible, and have carried the argument further in a book, which is now published as a companion volume to this, entitled *The Spontaneous Expansion of the Church and the Causes which Hinder it*. In that book I have tried to set forth the secret of an

[1] See *The Ministry of the Spirit*, World Dominion Press, 1960.

expansion which was a most remarkable characteristic of apostolic churches, and have examined the hindrances which have prevented us from establishing such churches.

If any of my readers desire to pursue the consideration of missionary methods further, I can only refer them to that book.

ROLAND ALLEN,
June 24, 1927   Beaconsfield

Contents

PART I

Antecedent Conditions

1 Introduction.

2 Strategic Points. *How far was St Paul's success due to the position or character of the places in which he preached?*

3 Class. *Was his success due to the existence of a special class of people to which he made a special appeal?*

4 Moral and Social Condition. *Was the moral, social or religious condition of the Provinces so unlike anything known in modern times as to render comparison between St Paul's work and ours futile?*

CHAPTER I

Introduction

In little more than ten years St Paul established the Church in four provinces of the Empire, Galatia, Macedonia, Achaia and Asia. Before AD 47 there were no churches in these provinces; in AD 57 St Paul could speak as if his work there was done, and could plan extensive tours into the far west without anxiety lest the churches which he had founded might perish in his absence for want of his guidance and support.

The work of the Apostle during these ten years can therefore be treated as a unity. Whatever assistance he may have received from the preaching of others, it is unquestioned that the establishment of the churches in these provinces was really his work. In the pages of the New Testament he, and he alone, stands forth as their founder. And the work which he did was really a completed work. So far as the foundation of the churches is concerned, it is perfectly clear that the writer of the Acts intends to represent St Paul's work as complete. The churches were really established. Whatever disasters fell upon them in later years, whatever failure there was, whatever ruin, that failure was not due to any insufficiency or lack of care and completeness in the Apostle's teaching or organization. When he left them he left them because his work was fully accomplished.

This is truly an astonishing fact. That churches should be founded so rapidly, so securely, seems to us today, accustomed to the difficulties, the uncertainties, the failures, the disastrous relapses of our own missionary work, almost incredible. Many missionaries in later days have received a larger number of converts than St Paul; many have preached over a wider area than he; but none have so established churches. We have long forgotten that such things could be. We have long accustomed ourselves to accept it as an axiom of missionary work that converts in a new country must be submitted to a very long probation and training, extending over generations before they can be expected to be able to stand alone. Today if a man ventures to suggest that there may be something in the methods by which St Paul attained such wonderful results worthy of our careful attention, and perhaps of our imitation, he is in danger of being accused of revolutionary tendencies.

Yet this is manifestly not as it should be. It is impossible but that the account so carefully given by St Luke of the planting of the churches in the Four Provinces should have something more than a mere archaeological and historical interest. Like the rest of the Holy Scriptures it was 'written for our learning'. It was certainly meant to be something more than the romantic history of an exceptional man, doing exceptional things under exceptional circumstances—a story from which ordinary people of a later age can get no more instruction for practical missionary work than they receive from the history of the Cid, or from the exploits of King Arthur. It was really intended to throw light on the path of those who should come after.

But it is argued that as a matter of fact St Paul was an exceptional man living in exceptional times, preaching under exceptional circumstances; that he enjoyed advantages in his birth, his education, his call, his mission, his relationship to his hearers, such as have been enjoyed by no other; and that he enjoyed advantages in the peculiar constitution of society at the moment of his call such as to render his work quite exceptional. To this I must answer: (1) That St Paul's missionary method was not peculiarly St Paul's, he was not the only missionary who went about establishing churches in those early days. The method in its broad outlines was followed by his disciples, and they were not all men of exceptional genius. It is indeed universal, and outside the Christian Church has been followed by reformers, religious, political, social, in every age and under most diverse conditions. It is only because he was a supreme example of the spirit, and power with which it can be used, that we can properly call the method St Paul's. (2) That we possess today an advantage of inestimable importance in that we have the printing press and the whole of the New Testament where St Paul had only the Old Testament in Greek. (3) That however highly we may estimate St Paul's personal advantages or the assistance which the conditions of his age afforded, they cannot be so great as to rob his example of all value for us. In no other work do we set the great masters wholly on one side, and teach the students of today that whatever they may copy, they may not copy them, because they lived in a different age under exceptional circumstances and were endowed with exceptional genius. It is just because they were endowed with exceptional

4

genius that we say their work is endowed with a universal character. Either we must drag down St Paul from his pedestal as the great missionary, or else we must acknowledge that there is in his work that quality of universality.

The cause which has created this prejudice against the study of the Pauline method is not far to seek. It is due to the fact that every unworthy, idle and slip-shod method of missionary work has been fathered upon the Apostle. Men have wandered over the world, 'preaching the Word', laying no solid foundations, establishing nothing permanent, leaving no really instructed society behind them, and have claimed St Paul's authority for their absurdities. They have gone through the world, spending their time in denouncing ancient religions, in the name of St Paul. They have wandered from place to place without any plan or method of any kind, guided in their movements by straws and shadows, persuaded they were imitating St Paul on his journey from Antioch to Troas. Almost every intolerable abuse that has ever been known in the mission field has claimed some sentence or act of St Paul as its original.

It is in consequence of this, because in the past we have seen missionary work made ridiculous or dangerous by the vagaries of illiterate or unbalanced imitators of the Apostle, that we have allowed ourselves to be carried to the opposite extreme, and to shut our eyes to the profound teaching and practical wisdom of the Pauline method.

Secondly, people have adopted fragments of St Paul's method and have tried to incorporate them into alien systems, and the failure which resulted has been used as an argument against the Apostle's method. For instance, people have baptized uninstructed converts and the converts have fallen away; but St Paul did not baptize uninstructed converts apart from a system of mutual responsibility which ensured their instruction. Again, they have gathered congregations and have left them to fend for themselves, with the result that the congregations have fallen back into heathenism. But St Paul did not gather congregations, he planted churches, and he did not leave a church until it was fully equipped with orders of ministry, sacraments and tradition. Or again, they have trusted native helpers with the management of mission funds, and these helpers have grievously misused them; but St Paul did not do this. He had no funds with which to entrust anyone. These people have committed

5

funds in trust to individual native helpers and have been deceived; but St Paul left the church to manage its own finance. These people have made the helpers responsible to *them* for honest management; but St Paul never made any church render an account of its finances to him. Or again, Europeans have ordained ill-educated native helpers and have repented of it. But they have first broken the bonds which should have united those whom they ordained to those to whom they were to minister, and then have expected them to be ministers of a foreign system of church organization with which neither the ministers nor their congregations were familiar. St Paul did not do this. He ordained ministers of the Church for the Church, and he instituted no elaborate constitution. When these false and partial attempts at imitating the Apostle's method have failed, men have declared that the apostolic method was at fault and was quite unsuited to the condition and circumstances of present-day missions. The truth is that they have neither understood nor practised the Apostle's method at all.

There is yet another and a more weighty reason: St Paul's method is not in harmony with the modern Western spirit. We modern teachers from the West are by nature and by training persons of restless activity and boundless self-confidence. We are accustomed to assume an attitude of superiority towards all Eastern peoples, and to point to our material progress as the justification of our attitude. We are accustomed to do things ourselves for ourselves, to find our own way, to rely upon our own exertions, and we naturally tend to be impatient with others who are less restless and less self-assertive than we are. We are accustomed by long usage to an elaborate system of church organization, and a peculiar code of morality. We cannot imagine any Christianity worthy of the name existing without the elaborate machinery which we have invented. We naturally expect our converts to adopt from us not only essentials but accidentals. We desire to impart not only the Gospel, but the Law and the Customs. With that spirit, St Paul's methods do not agree, because they were the natural outcome of quite another spirit, the spirit which preferred persuasion to authority. St Paul distrusted elaborate systems of religious ceremonial, and grasped fundamental principles with an unhesitating faith in the power of the Holy Ghost to apply them to his hearers and to work out their appropriate external expressions in them. It was inevitable that methods which were the natural outcome of the mind of St Paul should appear as dangerous to us as they appeared to the Jewish Christians of his own day. The mere fact that they can be made to bear a shallow resemblance to the methods of no method is sufficient to make the 'apostles of order' suspicious. In spite of the manifest fact that the Catholic Church was founded by them, they appear uncatholic to those who live in daily terror of schism. It seems almost as if we thought it uncatholic to establish the Church too fast.

But that day is passing. In face of the vast proportions of the work to be done, we are day by day seeking for some new light on the great problem how we may establish the Catholic Church in the world. In this search, the example of the Apostle of the Gentiles must be of the first importance to us. He succeeded in doing what we so far have only tried to do. The facts are unquestionable. In a very few years, he built the Church on so firm a basis that it could live and grow in faith and in practice, that it could work out its own problems, and overcome all dangers and hindrances both from within and without. I propose in this book to attempt to set forth the methods which he used to produce this amazing result.

I am not writing a book on St Paul's doctrine. I do not feel it necessary to argue over again the foundations of the faith. I am a churchman, and I write as a churchman. I naturally use terms which imply church doctrine. But the point to which I want to call attention is not the doctrine, which has been expounded and defended by many, but the Apostle's method. A true understanding of the method does not depend upon a true interpretation of the doctrine, but upon a true appreciation of the facts. About the facts there is very general agreement: about the doctrine there is very little agreement. E.g.— It is almost universally agreed that St Paul taught his converts the rite of baptism: it is very far from agreed what he meant by baptism. I use about baptism the terms of the Church of which I am a member. but my argument would be equally applicable if I used terms which implied a Zwinglian doctrine. Similarly I use about the orders of the ministry the terms natural to one who believes in apostolic succession. But the general force of my argument would not be affected if I used the terms natural to a Presbyterian or a Wesleyan. I suppose that I should scarcely need to alter more than a word or two, if I believed in 'the Churches' as firmly as I believe in 'the Church'. I hope, then, that, if I am happy enough to find readers who do not accept my ecclesiastical position, they will not allow themselves to be led away into the wilds of a controversy which I have tried as far as possible to exclude; and will rather seek to consider the method of the Apostle's work which I set forth than to find fault with the use of terms or expressions which imply a doctrine which they do not hold.

Neither am I attempting to describe the character of the Apostle or his special qualifications for the work, or his special preparation for it, still less am I attempting to write his life. I propose to deal simply with the foundation of the churches in the four provinces of Galatia, Macedonia, Achaia, Asia, in the ten years which covered the three missionary journeys. I wish to suggest an answer to the following questions:

I. Was there any antecedent advantage in the position or character of the cities in which St Paul founded his churches?

We must inquire:

(1) Whether he deliberately selected certain strategic points at which to establish his churches?

(2) Whether his success was due to the existence of some peculiar class of people to which he made a special appeal?

(3) Whether the social, moral or religious condition of the provinces was so unlike anything known in modern times, as to render futile any comparison between his work and ours.

II. Was there any peculiar virtue in the way in which the Apostle presented his gospel? Under this heading we must consider: (1) His use of miracles; (2) His finance; (3) The substance of his preaching.

III. Was there any peculiar virtue in the teaching which he gave to his converts or in his method of training his converts for baptism, or for ordination?

IV. Was there any peculiar virtue in his method of dealing with his organized churches? This will include the means by which (a) discipline was exercised and (b) unity maintained.

I shall try to point out as occasion offers where and how far we now follow or refuse the Apostle's method. It will, of course, be impossible and inadvisable to quote particular instances from the mission field. I can only deal in general terms with tendencies which will, I think, be quite familiar to any one who is acquainted with the missionary work of the present day.

V. Finally, I shall call attention to certain principles which seem to lie at the back of all the Apostle's actions and in which I believe we

8

may find the key to his success, and endeavour to show some at least of the ways in which the apostolic method might be usefully employed today.

CHAPTER 2

Strategic Points

It is quite impossible to maintain that St Paul deliberately planned his journeys beforehand, selected certain strategic points at which to establish his churches and then actually carried out his designs. The only argument, which seems to support that theory, is the use of the word 'the work' with regard to his first missionary journey in Acts 13. 2, 14. 26, 15. 38. In Acts 13. 2 it is said, 'The Holy Ghost said, Separate me Barnabas and Saul for *the work* whereunto I have called them'. In 14. 26 we are told that the apostles returned to Antioch 'from whence they had been committed to the grace of God for *the work* which they had fulfilled'. And in 15. 38 St Paul complains that Mark 'withdrew from them in Pamphylia and went not with them to *the work*'. These words taken together seem naturally to imply (*a*) that the apostles started out with a definite plan before them, (*b*) that they actually carried out their plans, and (*c*) that St Mark's fault lay in the fact that he had deserted a work which he had undertaken to do.

But the difficulties in the way of that interpretation are very great. If we accept Professor Ramsay's theory that the churches to which the Epistle to the Galatians was written were the churches in South Galatia, which St Paul founded on this journey, then there can be no dispute that St Paul did not design to visit them when he started out from Syria, for in that epistle he distinctly states that he preached to them because he was either driven to them or detained amongst them by an infirmity of the flesh.[1]

The most natural explanation of the return of John Mark from Perga is that he turned back because he saw that after the crisis at Paphos St Paul was become the real leader of the mission in the place of his own cousin, Barnabas, and was prepared both to preach outside the synagogue to Gentiles with greater freedom than he had anticipated, and to admit Gentiles into fellowship on terms which he was hardly proposing to accept. He saw too that St Paul was proposing to penetrate into regions more remote, perhaps more dan-

[1] Gal. 4. 13.

gerous, than he had expected. In other words there was at Perga a real change both in the direction and in the character of the mission.

On these grounds it seems more reasonable to suppose that the words 'the work' are used in a general sense of the objects of their journey rather than of any defined sphere of action. But whatever view we take of this first journey, it is perfectly clear that in the second journey St Paul was not following any predetermined route. If he had any definite purpose when he left Antioch it was to go through Cilicia and South Galatia to Ephesus. It is expressly stated that he tried to preach in Asia and was forbidden by the Holy Ghost, and that he then attempted to go into Bithynia and again was forbidden by the Spirit.[1] So he found himself at Troas not knowing where he was to go, until he was directed by a vision to Macedonia. Having preached in Philippi, Thessalonica and Beroea he was apparently driven out of Macedonia and fled to Athens[2] not, as it seems, with any intention of establishing himself there as a preacher, but simply as a retreat until circumstances would allow him to return to Macedonia. When he was expelled from Athens he went to Corinth, either because that was the most convenient place from whence to keep in touch with Macedonia, or because he was directed thither by the Spirit. In all this there is little sign of premeditation or deliberate design.

Only one other place remains at which St Paul established the church before his first imprisonment, viz. Ephesus, and it appears from Acts 18. 19 that he touched at that place in the ordinary course of his journey to Jerusalem, and that, finding the people ready to listen to him, he promised to return again.

On this third journey St Paul apparently laid his plans and executed them as they were designed so far as Ephesus, but after that he was so uncertain in his movements as to lay himself open to an accusation of vacillation.[3] It is during this journey that we find the first expressed plan for future work. Whilst at Ephesus, 'Paul purposed in the spirit when he had passed through Macedonia and Achaia to go to Jerusalem saying: After I have been there, I must also see Rome'.[4]

[1] Acts 16. 6, 7.
[2] Ramsay says that he 'left Beroea with no fixed plan'.—*St Paul the Traveller*, p. 234.
[3] 2 Cor. 1. 15, 18.
[4] Acts 19. 21.

I cannot help concluding then from this brief review that St Paul did not deliberately plan his missionary tours, but nevertheless there are certain facts in the history of his missionary journeys which demand attention.

1. Both St Luke and St Paul speak constantly of the provinces rather than of the cities. Thus St Paul was forbidden to preach the word in Asia,[1] he was called from Troas not to Philippi, or to Thessalonica, but to Macedonia.[2] Speaking of the collection for the saints at Jerusalem St Paul says that he boasted that Achaia was ready a year ago.[3] The suggestion is that in St Paul's view the unit was the province rather than the city.

2. Secondly, his work was confined within the limits of Roman administration. It is perfectly clear that in preaching in South Galatia, St Paul was evangelizing the Roman province next in order to his native province of Cilicia, in which there were already Christian churches. Between these two, there lay the territory of Lycaonia Antiochi, and across this territory St Paul must have passed when he went from Tarsus to Lystra and Iconium. Yet we are never told that he made any attempt to preach in that region. From this fact we must certainly infer that St Paul did deliberately consider the strategic value of the provinces and places in which he preached. The territory of Antiochus—Lycaonia Antiochi—was not so important from the view of the propagation of the Gospel as the region of Lystra. St Paul deliberately chose the one before the other.

3. Thirdly, St Paul's theory of evangelizing a province was not to preach in every place in it himself, but to establish centres of Christian life in two or three important places from which the knowledge might spread into the country round. This is important, not as showing that he preferred to preach in a capital rather than in a provincial town or in a village, but because he intended his congregation to become at once a centre of light. Important cities may be made the graves of a mission as easily as villages. There is no particular virtue in attacking a centre or establishing a church in an important place unless the church established in the important place is a church possessed of sufficient life to be a source of light to the whole country round.

[1] Acts 16. 6.
[2] Acts 16. 9, 10, cf. Acts 18. 5, 19. 22, 2 Cor. 1. 16, 2. 13, 7 5, Phil. 4. 15, etc.
[3] 2 Cor. 9. 2.

It is not enough for the church to be established in a place where many are coming and going unless the people who come and go not only learn the Gospel, but learn it in such a way that they can propagate it. It has often happened that a mission has been established in an important city, and the surrounding country has been left untouched so far as the efforts of the native Christians have been concerned, because the Gospel was preached in such a form that the native convert who himself received it did not understand how to spread it, nor realize that it was entrusted to him for that purpose. By establishing the church in two or three centres St Paul claimed that he had evangelized the whole province. Ten years after his first start from Antioch, he told the Romans that he had 'fully preached the Gospel of Christ from Jerusalem and round about Illyricum',[1] and that he had 'no more place in these parts'.[2] In that single sentence we have the explanation and the justification of St Paul's establishment of the churches in important centres in a province. When he had occupied two or three centres he had really and effectually occupied the province.

All the cities, or towns, in which he planted churches were centres of Roman administration, of Greek civilization, of Jewish influence, or of some commercial importance.

(1) Just as he refused to preach in native states and passed through large towns in the territory of Antiochus without stopping to preach, so within the Roman province he passed through native provincial towns like Misthia or Vasada in order to preach in Lystra and Derbe—military posts in which there was a strong Roman element. Professor Ramsay has shown that there is in the Acts an apparent intention to contrast the conduct meted out to St Paul by local provincial authorities with that which he received at the hands of Roman officials and to present the Romans in the light of protectors of the Apostle against the persecutions of the Jews.[3] No doubt in selecting as the sphere of his work the centres of Roman administration, St Paul was led by the desire to obtain for himself and for his people the security afforded by a strong government. He felt that as a Roman citizen he could in the last resort expect and receive the protection of Roman officials against the fanatical

[1] Rom. 15. 19.
[2] Rom. 15. 23.
[3] *St Paul the Traveller*, pp. 304 sqq.

13

violence of the Jews; but he did not only seek Roman protection. He found under the Roman government something more than peace and security of travel. He found not only toleration and an open field for his preaching, there was also in the mere presence of Roman officials an influence which materially assisted his work. The idea of the world-wide empire which they represented, the idea of the common citizenship of men of many different races in that one empire, the strong authority of the one law, the one peace, the breaking down of national exclusiveness, all these things prepared men's minds to receive St Paul's teaching of the Kingdom of Christ, and of the common citizenship of all Christians in it.

(2) The centres in which St Paul established his churches were all centres of Greek civilization. Even at Lystra, half the inscriptions which have been discovered are Greek, while the other half are Latin. Everywhere Roman government went hand in hand with Greek education. This education provided St Paul with his medium of communication. There is no evidence of any attempt to translate the Scriptures into the provincial dialects of Asia Minor.[1] St Paul preached in Greek and wrote in Greek, and all his converts who read at all were expected to read the Scriptures in Greek.[2] For St Paul, the one language was as important as the one government.

Moreover, the influence of Greek civilization was an influence which tended to the spread of general education, and Christianity from the very first was a religion of education. From the first, Christians were learners. They were expected to be able to give a reason for the hope that was in them. They were expected to learn something, if only a very little, of the Old Testament and of the stock proofs that Jesus was the Messiah. They were expected to know something of the life and teaching of Christ, and something of Christian doctrine. Before very long it became a common argument of the Christian apologists that amongst Christians, 'tradesmen, slaves, and old women knew how to give some account of God and did not believe without evidence'. It was from the widespread influence of Greek education that they were able to acquire this, and it was to places where that education was established that St Paul naturally turned.

[1] Ramsay, *St Paul the Traveller*, p. 132.
[2] Has this fact any bearing upon the multiplication of dialect Prayer Books, which tend to perpetuate divisions? E.g. in Chota Nagpur or the South Seas?

(3) Nearly all the places in which St Paul established churches were centres of Jewish influence. St Paul, as a Jew, was at home in the Jewry. He did not enter these great cities as a mere stranger. He came as a member of a family, as a member of a powerful and highly privileged association. Under the Roman Government the Jews enjoyed singular advantages. Their religion was definitely recognized. They had liberty to administer their common funds in their own way and to administer their own laws. They were exempt from the obligation to share in the worship of the Emperor, they enjoyed freedom from a military service in which it was evident they could not take part without violating their religion. They had many other privileges of less importance, but of considerable advantage.

When, therefore, St Paul took up his residence in the Jewry or entered the synagogue on the Sabbath Day, he had for the moment a singular opportunity. He had an audience provided for him which understood the underlying principles of his religion, and was familiar with the texts on which he based his argument. When he went out into the city, he went as a member of a community which was associated in the minds of all men with the idea of a very strict, if unreasonable, observance of religion. Men would naturally expect from him as a Jew an unbending stiffness towards every form of idolatry, and the unhesitating maintenance as a part of his religious system of a strict code of morals. Much as the Greek and Roman world disliked and spurned the Jew, yet the religion of the Jew was exercising a very wide influence and no small attractive power over the minds of some of the best and most thoughtful of the people.

(4) St Paul established his churches at places which were centres of the world's commerce. They were cities which occupied an important place as leaders of the provinces. They were foremost in every movement of policy or thought. They were sometimes almost ludicrously jealous of one another and strained all their powers in emulous rivalry to maintain their position as leaders. But they were leaders, and they felt it their duty to lead. They represented something larger than themselves and they looked out into a wider world than the little provincial town which was wholly absorbed in its own petty interests. Thus they were centres of unity, realizing that they had a responsibility for a world outside themselves. Even the settlers in Lystra and Derbe on the borders of a province realized that they

were pioneers of a civilization which they were to extend to the barbarous country round. They lived in a life that was larger than their own. They could not live wholly to themselves.

Nor were these cities only centres of their own provinces. Through some of them the commerce of the world passed. They were the great marts where the material and intellectual wealth of the world was exchanged. They were bound to the whole Empire by great roads of which they were the keys. In their streets the busiest and most fervent life of the Empire hurried to and fro. How constant that intercourse was we learn not only from the history of the early churches: we cannot forget that Phrygian, who in his single life made the journey from Phrygia to Rome no less than seventy-two times.[1] These places were not only centres of unity, they were points in the circumference of a larger unity.

Thus at first sight it seems to be a rule which may be unhesitatingly accepted that St Paul struck at the centres of Roman administration, the centres of Hellenic civilization, the centres of Jewish influence, the keys of the great trade routes.

We must not, however, allow ourselves to lay over-much stress on these characteristics of the places at which St Paul established his churches. They were common to a great many towns and cities on the great highways of the Empire. If the Apostle had gone to Laodicea or to Dyrrachium the same remarks might have been made about those places. In Macedonia, Beroea was not as important a place as Pella. St Paul plainly did not select where he would preach simply on grounds like these: he was led of the Spirit, and when we speak of his strategic centres, we must recognize that they were natural centres; but we must also recognize that for missionary work they were strategic centres because he made them such. They were not centres at which he must stop, but centres from which he might begin; not centres into which life drained but centres from which it spread abroad.

We have often heard in modern days of concentrated missions at great centres. We have often heard of the importance of seizing strategic points. But there is a difference between our seizing of strategic centres and St Paul's. To seize a strategic centre we need not only a man capable of recognizing it, but a man capable of seizing it. The seizing of strategic points implied a strategy. It is part

[1] Harnack, *Expansion*, trans. Moffatt. 2nd Edit. vol. i. p. 20, note 2.

of a plan of attack upon the whole country. Concentrated missions at strategic centres, if they are to win the province, must be centres of evangelistic life. In great cities are great prisons as well as great railway stations. Concentrated missions may mean concentrated essence of control or concentrated essence of liberty: a concentrated mission may be a great prison or a great market: it may be a safe in which all the best intellect of the day is shut up, or it may be a mint from which the coin of new thought is put into circulation. A great many of our best men are locked up in strategic centres: if once they get in they find it hard to get out. At many of the strategic points where we have established our concentrated missions it is noticeable that the church rather resembles a prison or a safe or a swamp into which the best life of the country round is collected than a mint or a spring or a railway station from which life flows out into the country round. We are sometimes so enamoured with the strategic beauty of a place that we spend our time in fortifying it whilst the opportunity for a great campaign passes by unheeded or neglected.

St Paul's centres were centres indeed. He seized strategic points because he had a strategy. The foundation of churches in them was part of a campaign. In his hands they became the sources of rivers, mints from which the new coin of the Gospel was spread in every direction. They were centres from which he could start new work with new power. But they were this not only because they were naturally fitted for this purpose, but because his method of work was so designed that centres of intellectual and commercial activity became centres of Christian activity. St Paul was less dependent upon these natural advantages than we generally suppose. We have seen that he did not start out with any definite design to establish his churches in this place or in that. He was led as God opened the door; but wherever he was led he always found a centre, and seizing upon that centre he made it a centre of Christian life. How he did this we shall see in the following chapters.

CHAPTER 3

Class

In these days there is a strong and apparently growing tendency to lay great stress on the importance of directing attention to some particular class of people in a country which we desire to evangelize. We had a striking illustration of the wonderful results which may be obtained by a judicious appeal to an influential class in the history of the 'Natural Foot Society' in China. The success of that movement was largely due to the fact that the promoters of the Society did not spend their time in preaching to the ignorant and conservative rustics of the villages, but began by enlisting the support of enlightened and well-to-do official and commercial families. As a consequence of that policy a movement started by a few foreigners became in ten or twelve years so firmly established in the country that foreign encouragement and support were no longer necessary.

Similarly, it was the appreciation of the value of a special class for the achievement of certain ends that led to the foundation of movements like the Student Christian Movement, and the same thought really lies at the back of nearly all educational missions in the foreign field as well as of special missions to official classes, whilst at the other end of the scale we are often told that in India we should concentrate all our efforts on the upraising of the depressed castes in the belief that the sight of the recovery and civilization of the most degraded and most despised will exercise an irresistible attraction over the other sections of society.

A common explanation of the success of St Paul's preaching in the Four Provinces is that he followed this method. There was, we are told, in the Four Provinces, a special class of people specially prepared for the reception and establishment of the Gospel, and it is used as an argument against the employment of St Paul's method in modern days under modern conditions that such a class does not now exist, and that our converts have none of the special advantages which his enjoyed. It is therefore important to inquire whether there was any special class to which he did in fact appeal, and whether the adherents which came to him from any special class were sufficiently numerous to justify us in rejecting his method, on the ground that that method was used by him under such peculiar circumstances, and applied by him only in dealing with converts of such special and peculiar character.

Is it possible to maintain that St Paul established Christianity in the Four Provinces by enrolling in its service the gifts and influence of any particular important class of men? This would scarcely appear to be the case. St Paul always began his work by preaching in the synagogue, to Jews and God-fearing Greeks. But neither Jews nor proselytes provided him with such a class. It very soon became apparent that Christianity could not take root in Jewish soil. The Christian spirit was in harmony rather with the freedom of the Greek mind than with the narrow legality of the Jewish. It was altogether too large to be bound by the shackles of Judaism. From the very first it was driven out of the nation in which it was born to find in a strange country not only its own life, but the life of those to whom it came. St Paul preached in the synagogue, indeed, but he was not allowed to preach there very long, nor did many Jews join themselves to him. It is not necessary here to examine the history of the founding of the church in the Four Provinces, it is not necessary to examine the epistles of St Paul to the churches in the Four Provinces, to show that those churches were composed almost entirely of Greek converts, for there is almost complete agreement on this subject. Again and again St Luke draws a sharp distinction between the obstinate refusal of the Jews, and the eager readiness of the Greeks to listen to St Paul's teaching. Again and again St Paul refers to his converts as men who knew idolatry by personal experience.

But St Paul's attempts to preach to the Jews were not only for the most part unsuccessful, they also stirred up great difficulties in his way. Not only did they invariably result in personal violence offered to him and sometimes to his converts, not only did they involve the sudden suspension of his work, whilst he fled for refuge from the fury which he had aroused; but they also brought into prominence a difficulty with which we today are only too familiar. They raised in the most acute form the question of the Apostle's own authority and the truth of his message. St Paul entered the cities as a Jew, and as a teacher of a form of Judaism. He claimed to be preaching a revelation given to men by the God of Abraham, Isaac and Jacob. He came to proclaim that the Messiah of the Jews was come, and had shown Himself to be not only the Saviour of the Jews, but of all men. Yet the moment he delivered this message the whole Jewish community rose up against him, expelled him, and sought to take his life as a blasphemer of God. Now if with us today the great stumbling-block in the way of our missions is the practical denial of Christianity, the indifference of men of our own blood, who yet call themselves Christians, this violent persecution of St Paul, by the religious teachers of his own nation, must have been a far greater stumbling-block; for it must have appeared to large numbers of people a sufficient refutation of the truth of his message. If from Jerusalem and round about to Illyricum St Paul had preached the Gospel, from Jerusalem and round about to Illyricum that Gospel was denied by all the people who were naturally best qualified to judge. When St Paul turned to the Gentiles it must have appeared that he had given up the attempt to convince the Jews, who really knew this Jesus of Nazareth, and that he was now wandering round the world, continually getting further from the place where the facts were known, trying to teach those who did not know something which those who did know rejected with scorn.

This difficulty would have been largely avoided if St Paul had not begun his preaching in the synagogue. It was when the Jews saw the multitudes, who had been worshippers in their synagogues, following the Apostle that 'they were filled with envy' and went about contradicting and blaspheming.[1] No doubt the difficulty was necessarily there and could not have been avoided, but by his preaching in the synagogue St Paul brought the difficulty at once to a head in its acutest form.

So it was that St Paul was constrained to advertise publicly the breach between himself and the Jews, proclaiming in the synagogue his severance from the Jews.[2] The tendency to do this became more marked as time passed, until he went so far as to force the attention of all men to the separation by opening his preaching-room next door to the synagogue.[3] This act of St Paul seems at first sight deliberately calculated to stir the passions of his countrymen,[4]—and

[1] Acts 13. 45; 14. 20; 14. 19.
[2] Acts 13. 46.
[3] Acts 18. 7.
[4] Ramsay, St Paul the Traveller, p. 256.

it is difficult to understand why St Luke should have called our attention to it so carefully, unless he had seen in it a distinct advance in the relation between St Paul and the Jews, between Christianity as represented by St Paul and Judaism.[1]

In order that Christianity might be fairly represented to the Greeks, it was necessary for St Paul to emphasize the truth that Christianity was not a sect of Judaism, and that its truth or falsehood was wholly independent of the attitude of Jewish authorities towards it. There may be thus some reason in the contention that St Paul preached first in the synagogue from a sense of religious obligation as much as from any motives of policy, and this seems to be the natural force of his words in the synagogues of Antioch[2] and Corinth[3] and his general attitude towards the Jews in the Epistle to the Romans. The preaching in the synagogue may have been a religious duty; it was certainly not an unmixed advantage. St Paul may have felt that he owed a debt to the Jews, but he can hardly be said to have deliberately aimed at the conversion of the Jews as a class.

Nevertheless, though St Paul did not make many Jewish converts in the synagogue, yet it was from the synagogue that he received a certain number of converts whose adherence must have been of great importance to the Church. Proselytes and God-fearing Greeks brought into the Church elements which were of the utmost value for the future life of the body. They had already an established conviction of the Unity of God and of the folly of idolatry. They possessed a conviction and experience of the necessity of morality for true religion. They had an acquaintance with the theory and practice of public worship and some knowledge of the Old Testament. St Paul was already using the Old Testament, not only as a textbook of controversy; he was also transferring it from the nation to which it naturally belonged to the new Israel to which it spiritually belonged. Already he was treating the story of Hagar as an allegory, already he was treating circumcision as a spiritual, not a carnal, rite, already he was proclaiming Abraham the father of the faithful. All this, some, at least, of the God-fearing Greeks were prepared to receive and understand and teach.

[1] It has been suggested to me that this incident has also some importance 'in view of present-day tendency to preach Christianity as a sort of "new way of Hinduism" '.

[2] Acts 13. 46.

[3] Acts 18. 6.

At the same time it is possible to exaggerate the influence which these people exercised in the Church. They cannot have been very numerous, for St Paul speaks of the majority of Christians in his churches as having been idolaters. The epistles to the Macedonian churches are the epistles which demand no acquaintance with the Old Testament for their understanding, and the moral warnings in those epistles refer to the vices which are common to heathen surroundings. When, then, we take it for granted, as we so often do, that the existence of a synagogue and the presence of some God-fearing Greeks in a city so alter the problem of church building that methods used by St Paul under these circumstances cannot possibly be applied to any modern conditions, I think we are labouring under a delusion. The existence of the synagogue and the presence of God-fearing Greeks enabled St Paul to receive into the church a few people who could read the Old Testament and were acquainted with the Law, a few people who were before dissatisfied with idolatry or heathen philosophy and were seeking after a truer and purer teaching. The Jews who joined St Paul had enjoyed this knowledge from their infancy, the Greeks who had become proselytes had enjoyed it for a few years. But this is not enough to justify us in imagining that the presence of these few people in a church made so vast a difference, that there can be no comparison between a church in which they were and a church in which they were not.[1]

Outside the synagogue St Paul does not seem to have addressed himself to any particular class. He certainly did not give himself up almost exclusively to preaching to the loafers, the porters, the ignorant and degraded, the casual labourers in the streets. He does not seem to have preached at street corners to the idle or curious crowd. It is true that the lame man at Lystra, who was apparently sitting by the wayside begging, heard St Paul speak. It is true that the soothsaying girl at Thessalonica had apparently heard him, and that we are told that he preached in the Agora at Athens, but whatever we may say with regard to the lame man at Lystra, it is by no means clear that the soothsayer at Thessalonica was doing more than

[1] Critics of the first edition said that I had underestimated here the importance of the converts from the synagogue. I have stated the case more fully in *The Spontaneous Expansion of the Church* and I have made a note on this point in the Preface to this Edition, and I have argued it in the form of a Dialogue on *The Establishment of the Church in the Mission Field*. (The second half of this dialogue is reprinted in *The Ministry of the Spirit* under the title, 'St Paul and the Judaizers'—Ed.)

repeating the popular estimate of St Paul and his preaching. At any rate, it is particularly stated that he was not preaching at the time, but was on his way to the place of prayer[1] where he was accustomed to preach. As for the Agora at Athens, that was certainly not what we ordinarily mean by the street corner. If then the fact that the lame man at Lystra heard St Paul speak necessarily implies that St Paul taught in the street, we must conclude that this was an exception to his general practice, for as a rule St Paul preached first in the synagogue and afterwards in the house of some man of good repute. It is curious how careful St Luke is to tell us exactly where St Paul lodged, or in whose house he taught, e.g. we are told that at Philippi he lodged with Lydia and preached at the prayer-place. At Thessalonica he lodged with Jason, and apparently taught in his house; at Corinth he lodged with Aquila, and preached in the house of Titus Justus; and at Ephesus he preached in the School of Tyrannus. St Luke evidently desires us to understand that St Paul was careful to provide things honest in the sight of all men, and took thought for what was honourable and of good report, as well as of what was true, and of what was pure, and of what was just.

On the other hand, St Paul did not seek particularly to attract the scholars, the officials, the philosophers. He certainly did not address himself to them. If he did so once at Athens, he deliberately refused to take that course at Corinth. He himself says that he did not receive many converts from those classes. 'From the middle and lower classes of society,' says Bishop Lightfoot,[2] 'it seems probable that the Church drew her largest reinforcements.' Similarly, Professor Ramsay declares that 'the classes where education and work go hand in hand were the first to come under the influence of the new religion'.[3] This conclusion is supported by St Paul's reference to the deep poverty of the churches of Macedonia;[4] and St Luke by his careful note of the conversion of 'chief women'[5] at Thessalonica, and of 'women of honourable estate'[6] at Beroea, seems to suggest that men of rank and importance were few. Moreover, the frequent references to slavery in the Epistles show that

[1] Acts 16. 16.
[2] *Ep to Phil.*, p. 20.
[3] *St Paul the Traveller*, p. 133.
[4] 2 Cor. 8. 1, 2.
[5] Acts 17. 4.
[6] Acts 17. 12.

many of the Christians belonged to that class. I conclude then that the majority of St Paul's converts were of the lower commercial and working classes, labourers, freed-men, and slaves; but that he himself did not deliberately aim at any class.

Moreover, it is difficult to believe that he did not also attract many people who make the least desirable converts. We are all familiar with the experience that people who are most ready to receive new impressions, to follow new ideas, to embrace new creeds, to practise new rites, are by no means always the most stable and admirable, sober and trustworthy, high-principled and honest-hearted of men. And one form of St Paul's preaching was of a kind peculiarly suited to attract many undesirable elements. Miracles draw a gaping crowd of idle, superstitious, and inquisitive folk. They make converts of those who are on the look-out for any means of gaining and exercising an influence over their fellows, people like the sons of Sceva, men who have a craving for power, without the natural ability which will enable them to win and exercise it in a natural way. They make converts of the weak-minded and credulous.

That many such did approach St Paul seems inevitable. If the churches of Galatia were anything like the churches of Achaia and Macedonia and Asia there were certainly many members whose ideas of religion and morality were far from high. St Paul did not exclude such. But he did not make his first converts of such. He so taught that no church of his foundation was without a strong centre of respectable, religious-minded people. These naturally took the lead and preserved the church from rapid decay.

Thus it would appear that St Paul made no attempt to seek after any particular class of hearers. He had his place of preaching and addressed himself to all who would listen, and, just as in China today,[1] men of different classes came in whilst he was preaching or called upon him for private conversation. His converts were no better and no worse than ours in any Eastern land. Not here is the secret of his peculiar success to be found. We cannot excuse our failure in the East on the ground that we have no synagogues to preach in, no proselytes to convert. If half our converts had been Jews or proselytes I think it would have made little difference. We have had plenty of good and able converts. In this St Paul had no advantage over us.

[1] This was written in 1912.

But it may be said that if this is true of the civilized East it is certainly not true of many other parts of the world. If St Paul's method of establishing churches is conceivably applicable to civilized peoples, it is certainly inapplicable to the uncivilized, the savage, the illiterate. To this, one answer is that we have never tried, and therefore cannot tell, what may be the power of the Holy Ghost in such cases.[1] But it is at least strange that we should hitherto have applied exactly the same rule to those whom no one ventures to call uncivilized and to those whom no one would call civilized. And further it is true that, where uncivilized men have accepted the Gospel, a very few years have wrought a most amazing change in their mental and moral outlook. They are often not incapable of education of the highest order, they are not destitute of natural ablity to lead, they are no mean evangelists. Examples can be found in the South Seas, in Papua, in New Zealand, in Central, South and West Africa, and among the low castes of India, in fact, everywhere. Is it true that the missions to the civilized people of the East are established more quickly or surely than those amongst the uncivilized? Our difficulty is that we have not yet tried St Paul's method anywhere, and have used the same argument to bolster up our dread of independence everywhere. For such an attitude St Paul's practice and the accounts of his work handed down to us lend no authority.

---

[1] I have argued elsewhere that St Paul's principles demand a method such as his everywhere and under all circumstances. His conception of Christ and of the Holy Spirit, of faith in Christ and of the grace of Christ, and of the power of the Holy Spirit, forbids any reliance upon Mosaic or philosophic teaching, or upon previous training of any kind, or upon any advantages enjoyed by any class of men before their conversion to Christ.

CHAPTER 4

Moral and Social Condition

The places at which St Paul established his churches were centres of Roman and Greek civilization. Now when we speak of Graeco-Roman civilization we generally have in mind the lofty teachings of the great philosophers, and we imagine a world permeated with those teachings. But as a matter of fact there was in the empire no common standard of civilization. The great cities were the homes of a bewildering variety of religions, and of an amazing assortment of people in every stage of civilization or barbarism. Their inhabitants differed one from another in manners and religion as widely as the Kaffir differs from the Englishman.[1] Dr Bigg tells us that the state of the empire in the first century can only be compared with the state of India since the conquests of Clive and Warren Hastings.[2]

This is a circumstance of the first importance when we turn to consider the moral surroundings of the churches founded by St Paul in the Four Provinces. We are sometimes apt to think that the social condition of those to whom St Paul preached may account for his success in establishing the Church, and the answer comes with irresistible force that the majority of St Paul's converts were born and bred in an atmosphere certainly not better, and in some respects even worse, than that with which we have to deal today in India or China.

There were of course lofty philosophies: there were profound mysteries: there were simple religious people like some of those whom Dion Chrysostom met in his wanderings. These are everywhere to be met in all ages, the people of profound thought or of simple faith; but such people were not really typical of the religion and morals of the Four Provinces in St Paul's day. They were no more typical than Chang Chih Tung was typical of the Chinese Mandarinate, or Tulsi Dâs typical of the Hindus, or Alfred the Great of the Saxons of his day. The Meditations of Marcus Aurelius were as far removed

[1] Bigg, *The Church's Task under the Roman Empire*, p. 2.
[2] *Ibid.*, p. 90.

from the religious life of the empire as the doctrines of Seneca were from his practice.

So Friedländer[1] contrasts the evidence afforded by the literature and the monuments of the early centuries of our era. 'The literature was chiefly the work of unbelievers or indifferentists, or of those who strove to spiritualize, purify or transform, the popular beliefs by reflection and interpretation. The monuments, on the other hand, to a great extent, at least, had their origin in those classes of society which were little affected by literature and its prevailing tendencies... thus in the majority of cases they are witnesses of a positive belief in a system of polytheism, of a faith which is free from doubt and subtlety alike.'

I cannot here, of course, attempt to depict the moral and social conditions of the provinces, but to a right understanding of St Paul's work it is essential that we should remember four elements in the life of the people.

(1) The first of these is the prevalence of belief in demons. 'In times of distress heathenism turned naturally to devil worship.'[2] 'Not merely idolatry, but every phase and form of life was ruled by them, they sat on thrones, they hovered round cradles, the earth was literally a hell.'[3] 'The whole world lieth in the Evil One.'[4] Not only Barbarians, not only Phrygians, but Romans, Greeks, and Jews all alike believed this. Not only the uneducated, but the most cultured were as fully persuaded of this universal power of devils as are the Chinese or the Gonds today. And the consequences of that belief were then what they are today—physical and psychical disease, cruelty, bondage, vice. Men like Pliny the Elder, who argued that it was the height of impiety to attribute to the gods adultery and strife and to believe in divinities of theft and crime, believed in the most horrible forms of magic. Human sacrifice was not unknown and belief in witchcraft was universal. Educated men believed that any enemy could practise in secret upon their lives by means of incantations. Plutarch was a good and learned man but he was quite serious, when, speaking of rites associated with unlucky and evil days, the devouring of raw flesh, mangling of bodies, fastings and beatings of the breast, obscene cries at the altars, ragings and ravings,

---

[1] Friedländer, *Roman Life and Manners*, Trans. J. H. Freese, vol. iii, p. 84.
[2] Bigg, *Neoplatonism*, p. 60.
[3] Harnack, *Expansion*, vol. i, p. 131.
[4] 1 John 5. 19.

he said that he did not suppose any god was worshipped with these rites, but that they were instituted to propitiate and keep off evil demons.[1] To this cause are to be traced the magic incantations of which so many have recently been found, and of which the formulae probably filled those magical books (worth 50,000 pieces of silver) which were publicly burnt at Ephesus under the influence of St Paul's preaching.

From this root spring the leaden tablets, the bits of bones, the belief in dreams and omens, the magical love-potions, the epitaphs on children carried away by spiritual beings, in a word, a whole world of abject superstition. When we read the treatises of the philosophers we think of religion in the empire as we think of religion in the East when we read the books of Sir Edwin Arnold or Mrs Besant. When we hear Dr Bigg tell us that 'it is probably not too hard a thing to say that demon worship was the really operative religion of the vast mass of the people of the empire',[2] we think of the religion of the empire as we think of the religion of the East when we read Dr Copleston's account of Buddhism in Ceylon, or Professor de Groot's description of the religion of the Chinese. Professor de Groot takes the lowest possible view of the character of Chinese religion, but whole chapters of his descriptions of Chinese demonolatry might be incorporated in Dr Bigg's or Dr Friedländer's account of popular religion in the empire without affecting in any way the general impression which those accounts are calculated to produce upon our minds.

Before conversion every one of St Paul's hearers was born and bred in this atmosphere of superstitious terror, and even after conversion the vast majority of them were still 'used to the idol' and did not cease to believe in demons. The preaching of St Paul and the other apostles was not a denial of this belief; it provided those who accepted it with invincible weapons wherewith to meet the armies of evil, but it did not deny the existence of those armies. It was only the scontant sense of the presence of the Spirit of Christ, before whom all spiritual powers must bow, that enabled Christians to banish these demons from their hearts and from the world in which they lived. Deliverance came not by denial but by conquest. Incidentally I should like to remark that in heathen lands it might still perhaps be the wiser course to preach constantly the supremacy of Christ over all

[1] *De fec. orac.*, xiv.
[2] *Church's Task*, p. 81.

things spiritual and material, than to deny or deride the very notion of these spirits. Some of our missionaries know, and it were well for others if they did know, that it is much easier to make a man hide from us his belief in devils than it is to eradicate the belief from his heart. By denying their existence or by scoffing at those who believe in them we do not help our converts to overcome them, but only to conceal their fears from us. By preaching the supremacy of Christ we give them a real antidote, we take to them a real Saviour who helps them in their dark hours.

(2) The second circumstance which it is impossible to ignore in considering the work of St Paul in the Four Provinces is the moral character of the religious rites. Some of the mysteries were no doubt capable of a highly moral interpretation. Harnack has collected in two or three pages the most important elements of the intellectual and religious tendencies in which the mingling of Hellenism and Orientalism prepared the way for the preaching of the Gospel.[1] 'The sharp division between the soul and the body, and the more or less exclusive importance attached to the spirit; the sharp division between God and the world, and the recognition that the Godhead is incomprehensible and indescribable yet great and good; the depreciation of the material world and of the body; the yearning for redemption from the world, the flesh and death; the conviction that redemption is dependent on knowledge and expiation; that life eternal is to be found in return to God, that the means are at hand and can be sought, that the seeker can be initiated into the secret knowledge by which the redemption is brought to him.' 'The soul, God, knowledge, expiation, asceticism, redemption, eternal life, with individualism and with humanity substituted for nationality—these were the sublime thoughts which were living and operative. . . . Wherever vital religion existed it was in this circle of thought and existence that it drew breath.' And he goes on, 'The actual number of those who lived within the circle is a matter of no moment. . . . The history of religion, so far as it is really a history of vital religion, runs always in a very narrow groove.'[2] But for our present inquiry the number of those who lived within the circle is a matter of first importance. A few elect souls understood a spiritual purpose in the mysteries of Ceres or of Isis or of Cybele; but, to the vast majority,

---

[1] Harnack, *Expansion of Christianity*, vol. i, pp. 31–3.

[2] Harnack, *Expansion*, vol. i, p. 33.

these rites did not suggest profound truths any more than the dancing and self-mutilation of the wandering priest—who made the round of the villages with his little shrine and idol and went through his performance of penance and expiation whilst a collection was being made on his behalf—suggested to the villagers any profound truths concerning sin and redemption. And the religious rites performed in the temples, both in respect of the filthy objects of devotion and the indecent concomitants of worship, were disgusting beyond all words. It is as impossible to quote the legends of the gods so worshipped, as it is to quote the stories of the Incarnations of Krishna, whilst the accompanying circumstances of the worship were only less filthy than the lives of the divinities in whose honour they were performed. Suffice it to say that the temples of Ephesus and Corinth were no more the homes of virtue than the temples in Benares or Peking. The language of St Paul in the Epistle to the Ephesians[1] exactly describes the condition of the people from whom his converts came, and amongst whom they lived.

It is upon these two conditions, superstition and uncleanness, that nearly all our arguments for our modern methods of conducting missionary enterprise in heathen lands today are based, and it is necessary that we should remind ourselves that, whatever may be the merits of St Paul's methods, they do not rest upon social and religious conditions superior to those under which most of our modern missions are conducted.

(3) But in addition to these there were two evils, the like of which are not now to be found throughout the world, slavery and the amphitheatre. It is not necessary here to repeat what is perfectly familiar to all men concerning the shows in the amphitheatre. What is more important for us is to note the attitude adopted even by the very best men towards these inhuman spectacles. Dr Bigg tells us that there are 'but three passages in which heathen writers express anything like adequate condemnation' of these shows.[2] And Friedländer says, 'In all Roman literature there is scarcely one note of the horror of today at these inhuman delights.'[3] For the most part they were spoken of with absolute indifference. People like Pliny and Cicero defended them as 'affording a splendid training for the

[1] Eph. 4. 17–19.
[2] *The Church's Task*, p. 117, note.
[3] Friedländer, *Roman Life*, vol. ii, p. 76.

eye, though perhaps not for the ear, in the endurance of pain and and as inspiring disdain of death and love of honourable wounds'. Even Marcus Aurelius was simply bored by them and complains that they were 'always the same'; whilst that model of Pagan virtue, Symmachus, was moved to bitter complaints by the heartless conduct of some Saxons who committed suicide in their cells rather than kill one another in public at the show which he had prepared in honour of his son's praetorship.

The extraordinary fascination which they exercised over the minds even of those who considered themselves far superior to such temptations is best illustrated by the oft-repeated tale of Alypius.[1]

Alypius was dragged into the theatre by some college friends. ' "If you drag me thither and put me there can you force me to give my eyes or put my mind to such a show?" he cried. "I shall be absent from it in spirit though present in body, and thus I shall overcome both you and it." When they had found their places he shut his eyes tight and forbade his thoughts to dally with such crimes. Would he could have sealed his ears also! For at some turn in the fight, the whole people broke into a roar of shouting, and overcome by curiosity, confident that whatever happened he could despise and forget even though he saw it, he opened his eyes. Then was he struck with a deadlier wound in his soul than the Gladiator whom he lusted to behold received in his flesh; and fell more miserably than the poor wretch over whose fall arose that bellow which pierced his ears and unlocked his eyes, and laid open his soul to the fatal thrust. . . . For, with the sight of blood, he drank in ruthlessness; no longer did he turn away, but fixed his gaze, and drank the cup of fury, and knew it not; he was fascinated by the din of battle, and drunk with murderous joy. He was no longer the Alypius who had come, but one of the crowd to which he had come, and the hardened accomplice of those who had brought him! Why should I say more? He gazed, he shouted, he raved, he carried home with him a frenzy which goaded him to return, not only with those who at first had dragged him thither, but before them dragging others in his turn.' 'No one,' says Tertullian, 'partakes of such pleasures without their strong excitements, no one comes under their excitement without their natural lapses.'[2]

---

[1] *Conf. Aug.*, Bk. vi. chap. 8, Dr Bigg's trans.
[2] Tert. *de Spec.* Ante-Nic. Lib., vol. xi, p. 23.

These shows had two very disastrous results: (1) They kept before all people's minds the division of humanity into two classes, men who had rights and men who had none, which was the great curse of slavery, and (2) this excitement made all other more reasonable forms of amusement seem tame. In particular they had a most disastrous influence over the theatre. 'What with the powerful excitement of the circus and the arena, the stage could only draw its audience by ignoble means, rough jokes and sensual by-play.'[1] Nothing was too gross, nothing too indecent, to be displayed in the theatre, nothing too sacred to be parodied there.[2] The legends of the gods often supplied the subjects of the most horrible and degrading scenes. 'When Bathyllus, a beautiful boy, was dancing, Leda, the most impudent actress of mimes, felt like a mere country novice on seeing such mastership in the art of refined sensuality.'[3]

Apuleius[4] describes a Pyrrhic dance which he saw at a festival at Corinth. There was a lofty mountain built of wood to resemble Mount Ida, covered with trees from which a fountain poured down a stream of clear water. A few goats were feeding on the grass and Paris, a young man dressed in flowing robes and crowned with a tiara, was tending them. Presently a beautiful boy, representing Mercury, whose only covering was a mantle thrown over his left shoulder, danced forward, holding in his hand a golden apple which he gave to Paris. Then a girl appeared dressed as Juno, having on her head a white diadem and carrying a sceptre. She was followed by another whom you could guess to be Minerva, for she had on her head a shining helmet encircled with an olive wreath. She raised her shield and brandished her spear like the goddess engaged in war. After these came another whose surpassing beauty and grace of colour proclaimed her to be Venus, and Venus in her youth. She was quite naked except for a transparent blue gauze scarf, with which the wind played lovingly. Her two colours, the white of her limbs and the blue of her scarf, showed that she was descended from the heavens and had come up from the sea. Juno, accompanied by Castor and Pollux, then danced with a quiet and unaffected grace and showed by gestures that she was offering to Paris the sovereignty

---

[1] Friedländer, *Roman Life and Manners under the Early Empire*, vol. ii, p. 90.
[2] See Arnobius, *Contra gentes*.
[3] Friedländer, *Roman Life*, vol. ii, p. 106.
[4] *Metam*, x, 30.

of Asia if he would give her the prize. Next Minerva, attended by Terror and Fear, who leaped before her brandishing drawn swords, rushed forward with tossing head and threatening glance, and showed by quick animated gestures that she would make him renowned for valour if he would give her the prize of beauty. Lastly Venus, who was greeted with loud applause, advanced with a sweet smile and stood in the middle of the stage surrounded by a throng of little boys so delicate and fair that they looked exactly like cupids just flown from heaven or from the sea. They had little bows and arrows and they carried torches before their mistress as if lighting her to the nuptial feast. Presently the flutes began to breathe soft Lydian airs which thrilled the audience with delight. But greater still was their delight when Venus began a slow sensuous dance which, to judge from his description, evidently appealed strongly to Apuleius. He particularly noted the play of her eyes, at one moment full of languor, at another flashing with passion. 'Sometimes,' he says, 'she seemed to dance only with her eyes.' She came before the judge and by movements of her arms was seen to promise that she would give him a bride of surpassing beauty like herself. He then gladly gave her the apple which he held in his hand in token of victory. After the judgment Juno and Minerva, sad and angry, retired from the stage, showing their indignation by their gestures. But Venus, full of joy and delight, showed her pleasure by dancing with all her choir. Then from some secret pipe in the top of the mountain there broke out a fountain of wine which filled the theatre with fragrance. Finally the whole scene disappeared into the ground sinking out of sight.

After quoting this story Friedländer proceeds to explain that these classic themes were altogether too refined for the vast majority. The chief delight of the educated was the pantomime; the common crowd preferred the boisterous rudeness and crude indecency of the mimes.

The moral influence of those spectacles in the circus, the amphitheatre or the theatre is more easily imagined than described. And it is not easily imagined. We instinctively beautify the past. We can hardly believe the descriptions of its vices. I suppose it is necessary to have lived long in intimate touch with heathen society to be able to understand at all what these things mean. But in the world today we can find no parallel to them. There are indeed vile religious plays, there are representations of divine beings, superhuman chiefly in their vices; but there are no gladiatorial shows, there are no criminals thrown to wild beasts.

(4) Finally there was slavery, and slavery in St Paul's days was very different from any slavery known to us, and that not for the better.

It differed from slavery in America or the West Indies in that the slaves of the Empire were of the same colour and very often of the same race, with the same education, as their masters. They were slaves today; tomorrow, if set free, they might take their place with perfect propriety and ease in the society of their master and mistress. There was no great barrier of blood, no great gulf of social habit or thought and cultivation.

In this it may, perhaps, be compared with slavery in China today. In China slaves are of the same colour and race as their masters, but there they are always of the lowest class and generally wholly uneducated. They are nearly all girls, and they are not a numerous class. But in the Empire the males were in a vast majority, and the numbers were appalling. Not only was the actual multitude of slaves in some of the great houses amazing, but the number of people living in some of the cities in whose families there was no servile taint, must have been comparatively small. Corinth was colonized by Caesar with freed-men. The whole fabric of society in the cities of the Empire was built upon slavery, and was penetrated through and through with that peculiar infection of slavery, servility and insolence. It is true that at this time the condition of slaves in the cities was somewhat mitigated. They were well educated often, and often kindly treated, but they had no rights. Women, girls and boys had no protection against their masters: their master's will was their only law of virtue. And there was nothing between any slave and the lash, except his master's will. Wealthy gentlemen, who had made their fortunes and secured their freedom, gave great sums to their physicians to remove the scars of the lash, or covered themselves with costly ointments to conceal them from the eyes of their guests.

Now consider for a moment the effect of these conditions on the education of those with whom St Paul had to do. From birth the child was in the care of a nurse who was a slave, 'steeped as a matter of course in the grossest and most horrible superstition'.[1] When he

[1] Bigg, *Church's Task*, p. 18.

34

was of age to go to school, the child was in the care of a pedagogue also a slave, whose interest it was to pander to his young master's vices, and to conceal his misdemeanours. He attended a private school kept by a freed-man. There he received an education which, Dr Bigg says, was admirably designed. The system of education adopted in the best of these schools was 'probably much better than any to be found in our own schools down to the time of Dr Arnold',[1] but it was thoroughly pagan. It is true that a great many of the best classical authors treat the legends of the gods as mere legends, and children in England read the stories of Jupiter, Venus and Aesculapius with no more sense of reality than they feel in reading the story of Bluebeard; but the children of St Paul's day were in a very different case. They read about Venus in Corinth beneath the shadow of the Temple of Venus with its 1,000 priestesses, whose deceits and arts were known to all the city. They read about Aesculapius with the knowledge that if they fell sick their parents would go to the Temple of Aesculapius to make an offering for their recovery. They read about Diana in Ephesus, where the silversmiths sold her shrines, and that impure image which fell down from Jupiter had its seat.

They understood a great deal too much; and the home influence was then, as ever in heathen lands, far from being what it ought to be. Even a good teacher could hardly counteract the influence of the nurse, the pedagogue and the parents,[2] and all teachers were not good teachers.

When he left the grammar school, if he could afford it, the child went to the teacher of rhetoric, where he learned to speak on any topic under any circumstances with grace, fluency, and at least an appearance of erudition. There were set problems and characters which the scholar discussed, and he learned not only to censure the adulterer, the pander, and the gamester, but to defend them. He learned also a nice judgment in all things literary. Then he went out into the world with this education in the history of the gods and the character of men, with the fear of demons as the one strong religious influence, if there was any strong religious influence at all; to attend the games, the circus, and the theatre, in which he found

[1] Bigg, *Church's Task*, pp. 5 and 6.

[2] '*Verba ne Alexandrinis quidem permittenda deliciis risu et osculo excipimus; nec mirum nos docuimus ex nobis audierunt. Nostras amicas, nostros concubinos vident; omne convivium obscenis canticis obstrepit, pudenda dictu spectantur*' is the complaint of Quintilian.

every possible incitement to his animal nature; to visit the temples on a feast day and to find them the homes of riot; whilst slaves were ever at his elbow ready to minister to his slightest wish. Every man of any education (except the Jews) in the churches of St Paul during these ten years had attended those schools, read that literature, visited those temples, and most of them had seen those games—and every Christian child of the parents who were St Paul's first converts passed through that same training. They received that education or they received none.

If the moral atmosphere in Greece was bad, in Asia Minor it was even worse. The character of the native religion was such that 'Greek education was pure in comparison, and the Greek moralists, philosophers and politicians inveighed against the Phrygian religion as the worst enemy of the Greek ideals of life. Greek society and life were at least founded on marriage; but the religion of Asia Minor maintained as a central principle that all organized and settled social life on the basis of marriage was an outrage on the free, unfettered divine life of nature, the type of which was found in the favourites of the great goddesses, the wild animals of the fields and the mountains. The Greek and Roman law which recognized as citizens only those born from the legitimate marriage of two citizens had no existence in Phrygian cities.'[1]

This is not, of course, a complete account of the social condition of the provinces in which St Paul preached; but these elements were there, and they cannot be ignored if we are rightly to understand the character of the task which lay before the Apostle. Devil worship, immemorial religious rites, gladiatorial games, slavery—these things cannot be set on one side. How can a man behave properly to his sick friend when he believes that he has a demon? How can the most lofty philosophic doctrines avail to produce rectitude when trouble sends a man to pray to a devil? How can a man preserve a true devotion and a reverent attitude towards the Divine, when the divinities known to him are described as the basest of creatures? How can a man walk aright when he and all his world take it for granted that there is a class of men, and that class the most numerous class, which has no rights of any kind, to whom nothing can be wrong which their master says is right, who were designed and created solely to give service and amusement to their owners, whether

[1] Ramsay, *St Paul the Traveller*, p. 138.

by their life or by their death? Professor Harnack tells us that 'it is a mistake to suppose that any "slave question" occupied the early Church. The primitive Christians looked on slavery with neither a more friendly nor a more hostile eye than they did upon the State and legal ties. They never dreamt of working for the abolition of the State, nor did it occur to them to abolish slavery for human or other reasons—not even amongst themselves.'[1] Large numbers of the members of the churches founded by St Paul were slaves, some of them were slave-owners. Christian masters are exhorted to clemency, Christian slaves to faithfulness. The fact that there was no 'slave question' simply emphasizes the universal acceptance of the conditions. What those conditions have always been wherever slavery has existed, what those conditions must have been where there was no colour or customary barrier between master and slave, is only too well known.

Whatever advantages of education, civilization, philosophy, religion, the Empire possessed, so long as it was defiled by slavery, the games, the temples and the magicians, it is, I think, impossible to argue that St Paul's converts had any exceptional advantages, in the moral character of the society in which they were brought up, which are not given to our converts today.

---

[1] *Expansion of Christianity*, vol. i, p. 167.

PART II

The Presentation of the Gospel

CHAPTER 5

Miracles

Miracles hold an important place in the account of St Paul's preaching in the Four Provinces, and, since this is one of the grounds on which is based the argument that his methods can have little or no bearing upon our work in the present day, it is necessary that we should examine carefully the nature and extent of these miracles, and the use which the Apostle himself made of them. We shall find, I think, that, so far from invalidating any comparison between his work and ours, St Paul's use of miracles may throw an interesting light upon some principles of constant value which should guide us in the practice of many forms of missionary enterprise common today.

Miracles are recorded of St Paul in five towns in the Four Provinces. In Iconium we are told that 'the Lord bare witness unto the word of His grace, granting signs and wonders to be done by their hands'.[1] At Lystra occurred the healing of a cripple.[2] At Philippi the expulsion of a spirit of divination,[3] and at Ephesus 'God wrought special miracles by the hand of Paul insomuch that to the sick were carried away from his body handkerchiefs or aprons and the diseases departed from them, and the evil spirits went out'.[4] Finally, at Troas occurred the recovery of Eutychus.[5]

This last miracle manifestly stands in a class quite by itself both in the nature of the case and in the surroundings in which it was wrought. It was not a miracle designed to further the proclamation of the Gospel: it was wrought for the comfort of believers, and it is to be compared rather with the raising of Dorcas by St Peter, than with the other miracles recorded of St Paul. It must therefore be left out of account in our present inquiry. At Antioch, Derbe, Thessalonica, Beroea and Corinth no mention is made in the Acts of miracles in connection with the preaching of the Gospel.

[1] Acts 14. 3.
[2] Acts 14. 8–10.
[3] Acts 16. 18.
[4] Acts 19. 11, 12.
[5] Acts 20. 9, 10.

Thus it would appear that the importance of miracles in the work of St Paul may be easily exaggerated. They were not a necessary part of his mission preaching: nor was their influence in attracting converts as great as we often suppose. Professor Ramsay indeed goes so far as to say that, 'The marvels recorded in *Acts* are not, as a rule, said to have been efficacious in spreading the new religion';[1] and it is true that only at Ephesus are we told of a great increase of disciples in close connection with the working of miracles, whilst in one case, at least, the working of a miracle was the immediate cause of serious obstruction.

But, on the other hand, the general tenor of St Luke's narrative certainly does not produce the impression that he considered St Paul's miracles other than as tending to further the cause of the Gospel. At Paphos a miracle led to the conversion of an important man; at Iconium signs and wonders were a witness to the truth of the Gospel; at Lystra a miracle introduced a great opportunity for expounding the doctrine; at Ephesus miracles were the means by which a great spiritual victory was won. St Luke does not speak of these as though they were not efficacious in spreading the Gospel. He rather speaks of them as though they were a natural and proper part of St Paul's ministry. He certainly does not relate all St Paul's miracles; for we know that St Paul wrought 'signs and wonders and mighty works' at Corinth (2 Cor. 12. 12). St Luke tells of some as typical of many.

There is, however, one sense in which the truth underlying Professor Ramsay's words illustrates a most important principle. These miraculous powers were never used by the Apostle to induce people to receive teaching. He did not attract people to listen to him with a view to being healed of disease, or by the promise of healing. It seems as if St Luke was careful to avoid producing the impression that miraculous powers might be used to attract people to accept Christianity because of the benefits which they might receive from it. We are never told of the conversion of anybody upon whom St Paul worked a miracle of healing. It is indeed true that the lame man at Lystra was apparently converted; but it is plainly suggested in the story that he was already in some sort a convert before he was healed. He was what a later age would have called a 'hearer', and his conversion as a result of the miracle is certainly not asserted. Neither

[1] *St Paul the Traveller*, p. 115.

are we told of the conversion of the soothsaying girl at Philippi. Bishop Lightfoot, indeed, and many others, take it for granted that she was converted. Referring to Lydia, the jailer, and this girl, he speaks of 'the three converts'.[1] This may be a legitimate inference, but it is certainly not a necessary one. St Luke tells us only that she proclaimed the apostles as servants of the Most High God, and that she was healed. We may think it impossible that such an event should take place in her life without leading to her conversion. It may have been so; but St Luke does not say that it was so.

St Paul did not convert or attempt to convert people by working miracles upon them. He did not attract people to Christianity by offering them healing. He did not heal on condition that they attended to his teaching. In this he was illustrating a principle which guided the Christian Church in her administration of charity throughout the early centuries of her history. 'We know,' says Professor Harnack, 'of no cases in which Christians desired to win, or actually did win adherents by means of the charities which they dispensed.'[2]

I cannot help thinking that this is a principle which we cannot be too careful to observe. There was a day in India when our missionaries paid a regular fee to scholars to attend our schools in order that they might receive Christian instruction. The result was not good, and that plan has been universally abandoned. But we still sometimes offer secular education, or medical treatment, as an inducement to people to submit themselves, or to place their children under our religious instruction or influence. This is, in principle, precisely the same thing as paying them, though in a far less vicious form. I cannot help thinking that the day is not far distant when we shall consider the offering of any material inducement as contrary to sound doctrine as we now consider the money payments of former days.

But if St Paul did not use his powers of healing as an inducement to people to receive his teaching, his use of miracles did yet greatly help him in his preaching. And that in four ways:

(1) His miracles attracted hearers. They were addressed rather to the crowd than to the individual. So it was at Lystra, so it was at the Beautiful Gate of the Temple, so it must ever have been. The

[1] *Ep. to Phil.*, Introd., p. 52.
[2] *Expansion*, vol. i, p. 386.

wonderful cures attracted men to St Paul. They came to see who it was that had done such a thing. They naturally were eager to hear what he had to say. So miracles prepared the way for the preaching.

(2) Miracles were universally accepted as proofs of the Divine approval of the message and work of him through whom they were wrought. A good illustration of this is to be found in the account given by Tacitus of the miracle wrought by Vespasian at Alexandria.[1] Two sick men at Alexandria were directed by the god Serapis to appeal to Vespasian for help. One was blind, the other had a crippled hand. The one begged Vespasian to anoint his cheeks and eyes with spittle, the other prayed that he would put his foot upon him. Vespasian at first laughed at them and put them aside; but at last he was persuaded to do what they desired. Instantly the hand of the one was restored and the blind received his sight. 'People,' says Tacitus, 'who were present at the scene still tell the story though there is now no advantage to be gained by lying.' And he remarks that these miracles were tokens of divine favour and affection for Vespasian. Everywhere by all men the same conclusion was drawn from the power to work wonders. So St Luke insists that the signs and wonders wrought by St Paul at Iconium were a witness given by God to the word of His grace. So amongst the Jews Christ Himself frequently appealed to His works; so Nicodemus confessed, 'No man can do these signs that Thou doest except God be with him'. So the blind man healed by Christ expressed the common belief when he declared, 'We know that God heareth not sinners', and many hearing of that case said, 'How can a man that is a sinner do such signs?' And this belief continued amongst the Christians. A most remarkable testimony of the appeal to miracles is found in the account of the Council held at Jerusalem to discuss the question of the admission of Gentiles to the Church. The question was raised whether the work of Paul and Barnabas was in accordance with the will of God. St Peter, we are told, prepared the minds of the assembled multitude by reminding the Council how he himself (a man of whose orthodoxy there could be no doubt) had been led by the Holy Ghost to preach to Gentiles, and then Barnabas and Paul rose to address the Council. Now it had been expressly remarked that throughout their journey to Jerusalem they had been declaring to the Christians at every place, 'How God had opened the door of

[1] Tac., *Hist.*, iv, 81.

faith unto the Gentiles', and 'the conversion of the Gentiles'.[1] But in the Council the point upon which the apostles laid stress was not this but their miracles. 'All the multitude,' it is said, 'kept silence; and they hearkened unto Barnabas and Paul rehearsing what signs and wonders God had wrought among the Gentiles by them'.[2] That the Gentiles had been converted, that they had embraced the Gospel, that they had suffered persecution, that they were devoted followers of Jesus Christ, these things might satisfy the apostles; but for the multitude the one convincing proof of God's approval of their action was that He had enabled them to work miracles.

In exactly the same way when he wishes to persuade the Galatians of the superiority of the Gospel to the Law, St Paul appeals to the evidence of miracles, 'He therefore that supplieth to you the spirit, and worketh miracles among you, doeth he it by the works of the law, or by the hearing of faith?'.[3] So too, when he is laying before the Corinthians the evidence of his apostleship, he appeals to miracles. 'Truly the signs of an apostle were wrought among you in all patience by signs and wonders and mighty works.'[4]

For Christian, and Jew, and pagan alike the evidence from miracles was irresistible. Given the miracle, the approval of the god in whose name the miracle was done followed as a necessary consequence.

(3) Miracles were illustrations of the character of the new religion. They were sermons in act. They set forth in unmistakable terms two of its fundamental doctrines, the doctrine of charity and the doctrine of salvation, of release from the bondage of sin and the power of the devil.

Charity, pity for the weak and the oppressed, love for men expressed in deed and word, as taught by Christ and His apostles, and as practised by them, was something quite new in the history of the world. Christ not only gave men the parable of the Good Samaritan and the oft-repeated command: He went about doing good. He first inspired men with the spirit of charity. He first opened their eyes to see in every case of trouble and disease, not a loathsome thing to be avoided, but an opportunity for the revelation of grace and loving-kindness. Inspired by that spirit St Paul uttered his profoundest

[1] Acts 14. 27; 15. 3.
[2] Acts 15. 12.
[3] Gal. 3. 5.
[4] 2 Cor. 12, 12.

45

teaching on the power of charity. 'Though I speak with the tongues of men and of angels and have not charity, I am become as sounding brass and tinkling cymbal.' In that spirit he worked his miracles. Heathen magicians, for a great price, exercised their powers, uttered their incantations, administered their potions. St Paul healed the sick and cast out devils because he was grieved at the bitter bondage of the oppressed or because he welcomed with the insight of sympathy the first signs of a faith which could respond to the power of the Lord. In this respect his miracles were the first steps in the path by which the early Church became renowned amongst the heathen for its organized charity, its support of widows and orphans, its tender care for the sick, the infirm and disabled, its gentle consideration for slaves, its constant help afforded to prisoners and those afflicted by great calamities. Two centuries later Tertullian, after recounting the charities of the Christians, could write, 'It is mainly the deeds of a love so noble that lead many to put a brand upon us'.[1] How great and powerful an assistance this was to the conversion of the world is known to all men.

(4) Similarly, St Paul's miracles illustrated the doctrine of release, of salvation. In the world to which the apostles preached their new message, religion had not been the solace of the weary, the medicine of the sick, the strength of the sin-laden, the enlightenment of the ignorant: it was the privilege of the healthy and the instructed. The sick and the ignorant were excluded. They were under the bondage of evil demons. 'This people which knoweth not the law are accursed,'[2] was the common doctrine of Jews and Greeks. The philosophers addressed themselves only to the well-to-do, the intellectual and the pure. To the mysteries were invited only those who had clean hands and sound understanding. It was a constant marvel to the heathen that the Christians called the sick and the sinful.

> Every one, they say, who is a sinner, who is devoid of understanding, who is a child, and, to speak generally, whoever is unfortunate, him will the Kingdom of God receive. Do you not call him a sinner, then, who is unjust, and a thief, and a housebreaker, and a poisoner, and a committer of sacrilege, and a robber of the dead? What others would a man invite, if he were issuing a proclamation for an assembly of robbers?[3]

[1] Tert., *Ap.* 39. Ante-Nic. Libr. vol. xi, p. 119.
[2] St John 7. 49.
[3] *Orig. c. Cels.* iii, lix, trans. by Crombie. Ante-Nic. Libr. vol. xxiii, p. 139.

Nevertheless, there was at this time a growing sense of need. Men were seeking in religion for healing and salvation. The cult of Aesculapius as 'the Saviour' was already spreading widely amongst the people and other gods too were called saviours. 'No one,' says Harnack, 'could be a god any longer unless he was also a saviour.'[1] Men were prepared to welcome a doctrine of salvation. It was to this sense of need that the Apostle appealed. 'The loving-kindness of God our Saviour hath appeared unto all men.'[2] His preaching was 'the power of God unto salvation to every one that believeth;' his converts were turned 'from darkness to light, and from the power of Satan unto God'. Into a world burdened with sin and misery and death he came in the Spirit of Jesus who went about doing good and healing all that were oppressed of the devil. His miracles were a visible sign to the whole world of the nature and purpose of his teaching. They proclaimed Jesus as the deliverer of the captives, the healer of the sick, the solace of the weary, the refuge of the oppressed.

There can be no doubt that this power of working marvels, this striking demonstration of the authority of Jesus over evil spirits, was in the early Church considered to be a most valuable weapon with which to confute opponents and to convince the hesitating. 'It was as exorcisers,' says Professor Harnack, 'that the Christians went out into the great world, and exorcism formed one very powerful method of their mission propaganda.'[3] Every Christian apologist appeals to it as a signal proof of the superiority of Christianity over heathen religions. The heathen appealed to miracles, to oracles, to portents, as proofs of the existence of the gods; Christians appealed to exorcism as proof of the divinity of Christ and of His superior authority over all the heathen gods and demons.

Such powers were highly valued in the Church and greatly coveted by the faithful. But their importance can be easily over-rated and it is manifest that St Paul saw this danger and combated it. He does not give the gift of miracles the highest place amongst the gifts of the Spirit. He does not speak as if the best of his workers possessed it. It was not the power of working miracles which was of importance in his eyes: it was the Spirit which inspired the life. Miraculous power was only one of many manifestations of the

[1] *Expansion*, vol. i, p. 107
[2] Titus 3. 4.
[3] *Expansion*, vol. i, p. 131.

47

Spirit; above all, best of all, is the spirit of charity. It was not the manner in which the healing was wrought, by a word instantly, which was of value in his eyes: it was the demonstration of the Spirit and of power.

Every day we see how it is not the possession of great powers but rather the spirit in which any power is used which attracts, which moves, which converts. If we no longer possess his power we still possess the Spirit which inspired him. We have powers enough whereby to let the Spirit shine forth. We have powers sufficient to gather hearers; we have powers sufficient to demonstrate the Divine Presence of the Spirit of God with us; we have powers sufficient to assure inquirers of the superiority of Christianity to all heathen religions; we have powers sufficient to illustrate in act the character of our religion, its salvation and its love, if only we will use our powers to reveal the Spirit. One day we shall perhaps recover the early faith in miracles. Meanwhile, we cannot say that the absence of miracles puts an impassable gulf between the first century and today, or renders the apostolic method inapplicable to our missions. To say that were to set the form above the spirit.

CHAPTER 6

Finance

It may at first sight seem strange to speak of finance as one of the external accompaniments of the preaching, rather than as part of the organization of the Church. But it is as it affects St Paul's approach to his hearers that finance assumes its real significance and throws its most interesting light upon our missionary work today. The primary importance of missionary finance lies in the fact that financial arrangements very seriously affect the relations between the missionary and those whom he approaches. It is of comparatively small importance how the missionary is maintained: it is of comparatively small importance how the finances of the Church are organized: what is of supreme importance is how these arrangements, whatever they may be, affect the minds of the people, and so promote, or hinder, the spread of the Gospel.

By modern writers this is often overlooked, and the finance of St Paul's journeys is treated as an interesting detail of ancient history, not as though it had anything to do with his success as a preacher of the Gospel. St Paul himself does not so treat it. It is strange how often he refers to it, what anxiety he shows that his position should not be misunderstood; but he speaks as if its importance lay wholly in the way in which it might affect those to whom he preached, never as though it made any personal difference to him.

There seem to have been three rules which guided his practice: (1) That he did not seek financial help for himself; (2) that he took no financial help to those to whom he preached; (3) that he did not administer local church funds.

(1) He did not seek financial help. In his first contact with strangers and in his dealings with the Church he was careful to avoid any appearance of money making. Amongst the heathen there was a large class of teachers who wandered from town to town collecting money from those who attended their lectures. There was also a large class of people who wandered about as mystery-mongers, exhibiting their shows and collecting money from those who attended

them. For these men philosophy and religion were a trade. St Paul would not be accounted as one of them. He refused to receive anything from those who listened to him. Similarly in the Church there was a class of people who made their living by preaching. St Paul did not condemn these; on the contrary, he argued that it was legitimate that they should do so.[1] Heathen religion, the Jewish law, Christ's directions, all alike insisted on the right of the minister to receive support. But he himself did not receive it, and he was careful to explain his reason. He saw that it would be a hindrance to his work. 'We bear all things,' he says, 'that we may cause no hindrance to the Gospel of Christ.'[2] He was anxious to show his fatherly care for his disciples by refusing to burden them with his maintenance. 'As a nurse cherisheth her children, we were well pleased to impart unto you not the Gospel of God only, but also our own souls, because ye were become very dear unto us.'[3] 'For ye remember, brethren, our labour and travail: working night and day, that we might not burden any of you, we preached unto you the Gospel of God.'[4] He was anxious to set them an example of quiet work, 'We did not behave ourselves disorderly among you: neither did we eat any man's bread for nought'.[5] 'But above all he was anxious to avoid any appearance of covetousness,'[6] and 'What I do, that I will do, that I may cut off occasion from them which desire an occasion.'[7] So, too, in his last speech to the Ephesian elders he lays great stress on the fact that he had not made money by his preaching, but had supported himself by the labour of his own hands. 'I coveted no man's gold or apparel. Ye yourselves know that these hands ministered unto my necessities.'[8]

---

[1] When I wrote this book I had not observed that in addressing the Elders of Ephesus St Paul definitely directs them to follow his example and to support themselves (Acts 20. 34, 35). The right to support is always referred to wandering evangelists and prophets, not to settled local clergy (see St Matt. 10. 10; St Luke 10. 7; 1 Cor. 9. 1–14) with the doubtful exceptions of Gal. 6. 6 and 1 Tim. 5. 18, and even if those passages do refer to money gifts, they certainly do not contemplate fixed salaries which were an abomination in the eyes of the early Christians, see Euseb. H.E. v. 18, 2.

[2] 1 Cor. 9. 12.
[3] 1 Thess. 2. 7, 8.
[4] 1 Thess. 2. 9.
[5] 2 Thess. 3. 7, 8.
[6] 1 Thess 2. 5.
[7] 2 Cor. 11, 12.
[8] Acts 20. 33, 34.

Yet St Paul did receive gifts from his converts. He speaks of the Philippians as having sent once and again unto his necessity,[1] and he tells the Corinthians that he 'robbed other churches, taking wages of them, that he might minister to them'.[2] He does not seem to have felt any unwillingness to receive help; he rather welcomed it. He was not an ascetic. He saw no particular virtue in suffering privations. The account of his journeys always gives us the impression that he was poor, never that he was poverty-stricken. He said indeed that he knew how 'to be in want', 'to be filled, and to be hungry'.[3] But this does not imply more than that he was in occasional need. Later, he certainly must have had considerable resources, for he was able to maintain a long and expensive judicial process, to travel with ministers, to gain a respectful hearing from provincial governors, and to excite their cupidity. We have no means of knowing whence he obtained such large supplies; but if he received them from his converts there would be nothing here contrary to his earlier practice. He received money; but not from those to whom he was preaching. He refused to do anything from which it might appear that he came to receive, that his object was to make money.

In this our modern practice is precisely the same. Our missionaries all receive their supplies from home, and cannot possibly be thought to seek financial support from their converts. If they ever seem to be preaching for the sake of their living, that can only be because their attitude towards the preaching gives some cause or occasion for the charge.

(2) Secondly, St Paul not only did not receive financial aid from his converts, he did not take financial support to his converts. That it could be so never seems to have suggested itself to his mind. Every province, every church, was financially independent. The Galatians are exhorted to support their teachers.[4] Every church is instructed to maintain its poor. There is not a hint from beginning to end of the Acts and Epistles of any one church depending upon another, with the single exception of the collection for the poor saints at Jerusalem. That collection had in the mind of St Paul a very serious and important place, but it had nothing to do with church finance in the

[1] Phil. 4, 16.
[2] 2 Cor. 11. 8.
[3] Phil. 4. 12.
[4] Gal. 6. 6.

ordinary sense. Its importance lay in its demonstration of the unity of the church, and in the influence which such a proof of brotherly charity might have in maintaining the unity of the church. But it had no more to do with church finance in the ordinary sense of the word than a collection made in India for Christians suffering from famine in China would have to do with ordinary Indian Church finance. That one church should depend upon another for the supply of its ordinary expenses as a church, or even for a part of them, would have seemed incredible in the Four Provinces.

From this apostolic practice we are now as far removed in action as we are in time. We have indeed established here and there churches which support their own financial burdens, but for the most part our missions look to us for very substantial support, and it is commonly taken for granted that every new station must do so, at any rate for some considerable time. Our modern practice in founding a church is to begin by securing land and buildings in the place in which we wish to propagate the Gospel, to provide houses in which the missionary can live, and a church, or at least a room, fitted up with all the ornaments of a Western church, in which the missionary may conduct services, sometimes to open a school to which we supply the teachers. The larger the establishment and the more liberally it is supplied with every possible modern convenience, the better we think it suited to our purpose. Even in the smallest places we are anxious to secure as speedily as possible land on which to build houses and churches and schools, and we take it for granted that the acquirement of these things by the foreign missionary, or by the foreign society, is a step of the first importance. Since it is obviously impossible that the natives should supply all these things, even if they are anxious to receive our instruction, it naturally follows that we must supply them. Hence the opening of a new mission station has become primarily a financial operation, and we constantly hear our missionaries lament that they cannot open new stations where they are sorely needed, because they have not the necessary funds to purchase and equip the barest missionary establishment.

This habit of taking supplies with us is due chiefly to two causes: first, the amazing wealth of the church at home and the notion that reverence and devotion depend upon the use of expensive religious furniture to which our luxury has accustomed us, and, secondly, the prevalence of the idea that the stability of the church in some way depends upon the permanence of its buildings. When we have secured a site and buildings we feel that the mission is firmly planted; we cannot then be easily driven away. A well-built church seems to imply a well-founded, stable society. So the externals of religion precede the inculcation of its principles. We must have the material establishment before we build the spiritual house.

As we begin, so we go on. Hence the frequent appeals to be found in church newspapers for organs and bells, cassocks, surplices and candlesticks, and such like, for mission stations in India or in Africa. How can we teach the new converts the majesty of worship without the materials for dignified ceremonial? Dignified ceremonial is ceremonial as practised in the best churches at home. The best churches use these things. The natives cannot supply them. It follows that we must take these gifts to our converts.

Thus, the foundation of a new mission is primarily a financial operation. But it ought not properly to be a financial operation, and the moment it is allowed to appear as such, that moment very false and dangerous elements are introduced into our work.

(i) By our eagerness to secure property for the church we often succeed in raising up many difficulties in the way of our preaching. We sometimes, especially perhaps in such a country as China, arouse the opposition of the local authorities who do not desire to give foreigners a permanent holding in their midst. We occasionally even appeal to legal support to enforce our right to purchase the property, and thus we begin our work in a turmoil of strife and excitement which we might have avoided.

(ii) We load our missionaries with secular business, negotiations with contractors, the superintendence of works, the management of a considerable establishment, to which is often added anxiety about the supply of funds for providing and maintaining the establishment. In this way their attention is distracted from their proper spiritual work, their energy and power is dissipated, and their first contact with the people whom they desire to evangelize is connected with contracts and other purely secular concerns. It is sad to think what a large proportion of the time of many of our missionaries is spent over accounts. It is sad to sit and watch a stream of Christian visitors calling upon a missionary, and to observe that in nearly every case the cause which brings them is money. They are the financial agents of the mission.

(iii) But in creating these missionary establishments we not only overburden our missionaries with secular business, we misrepresent our purpose in coming to the place. It is of the utmost importance that the external manifestation of our purpose should correspond with the inward intention and rightly express it. We live in a world in which spirit is known through material media. When the Son of God desired to reveal Himself to us, He took upon Him the form of a servant, and He made a material body the manifestation to all men of the Eternal God who is Spirit. That fact must govern all our thought. That is why the religion of Christ, who is Himself a Sacrament, is sacramental, and all our use of material things is sacramental. We, in our measure, do what He did. I know nothing of missionary zeal except as expressed in words and gifts and deeds. We cannot express ourselves otherwise in this world. Desire must employ words and glances and such like material vehicles. That is the reason why material apparatus is capable of spiritual uses. In themselves words and buildings have no power to produce spiritual results. If we will not preach we cannot convert, but no preaching in itself can convert. The value of the outward things is derived from the spirit which animates them and gives them being. They are manifestations of the Spirit of Christ who desires the salvation of men, working in us. It is the Spirit of Christ indwelling us who operates through them. Therefore, that external instrument is best which reveals the Spirit. The Body of Jesus was such an instrument: the Sacraments ordained by Christ are such. The Sacraments of the Gospel are not contrary to nature, but they are Divine.

A method of working, or a material instrument, may reveal or conceal, or misrepresent, the Spirit: e.g. in France the offer of the left hand is an act of cordial goodwill; in India it is an insult. If then a Frenchman in India were to offer a man his left hand, his goodwill would be interpreted as illwill. In ignorance we may use unsuitable expressions, but the moment we become aware that they are unsuitable we can no longer use them. That is why reformers constantly reject the use of things which have been long employed as the expressions of a spirit which they do not want to express. They must alter the form of the sacrament in order to reveal the change in their point of view. Today in India many of our younger missionaries are beginning to revolt against the big bungalows used by their pre-decessors. They look at them and say, 'That does not quite represent the spirit in which I wish to approach these people'. If that feeling grows, they must sooner or later abandon the bungalow. For if we are persuaded that the material vehicle misrepresents the spirit which we would express, and yet continue to use it, it checks the spirit in us. If we want to express respect and goodwill we cannot continue to offer the left hand, when we know that it will certainly be misunderstood. If we do so, we do violence to our feeling of goodwill, and our goodwill is checked and injured.

Moreover, because we cannot express ourselves, cannot manifest our real purpose in them, the use of wrong materials repels those whom we might draw to us. All men everywhere judge the inward spirit by the external form, and are attracted or repelled by it. They are apt to be much influenced by the first glance. If, then, the material form really does not express the true spirit, we cannot be surprised if they are hindered.

Now the purchase of land and the establishment of foreign missions in these establishments, especially if they are founded in the face of opposition from the local authorities, naturally suggest the idea of a foreign domination. The very permanence of the buildings suggests the permanence of the foreign element. The land is secured, and the buildings are raised, in the first instance by the powerful influence of foreigners. That naturally raises a question in the native mind why these people should be so eager to secure a permanent holding in their midst. They naturally suspect some evil ulterior motive. They suppose that the foreigner is eager to extend his influence and to establish himself amongst them at their expense. In China, particularly, the common idea prevalent amongst the people is that to become a Christian involves submission to foreign domination. This conception has a most powerful effect in deterring the people from approaching the missionary or from receiving his teaching with open minds. I think it is now almost universally admitted that the permanence of foreign rule in the Church ought not to be our object in propagating the Gospel. But by taking large supplies with us to provide and support our establishments and organizations we do in fact build up that which we should be most eager to destroy.

Moreover, we do not want to produce the impression that we design to introduce an institution, even if it is understood that the institution is to be naturalized. Christianity is not an institution, but a principle of life. By importing an institution we tend to obscure the truly spiritual character of our work. We take the externals first and so we make it easy for new converts to put the external in the place of the internal. Attendance at a house of prayer may take the place of prayer. It is easy to mistake the provision of the ornaments of worship for the duty of worship. The teachers seem to think these things so important that they must be the really important things. The duty of the Christian is to learn to attend to these things, and to go through the proper forms. The heathen naturally looks at religion from that point of view, and when he sees the externals provided at a cost which seems to him very great, and things imported which the country cannot provide, he inevitably tends to suppose that our religion is as his own, and the organization and the institution take just that place in his thought which was formerly occupied by his own organization and institutions of religion. But this is precisely what we want to avoid.

Nor is this all. The first glance at these missions financed from abroad naturally suggests that the religion which they represent is foreign. They are supported by foreign money, they are often foreign in appearance. Eastern people almost universally look upon Christianity as a foreign religion, and they do not want a foreign religion. This is one of the very chiefest and most insidious of our difficulties. We are not the preachers of a Western religion, and anything which tends to create or support that misunderstanding is a thing rather to be avoided than encouraged. By the introduction of Western buildings and Western religious furniture we can hardly avoid strengthening that misunderstanding. Of course, if we are prepared to maintain that our Western ornaments are essentially Catholic and must be adopted everywhere as integral parts of the Catholic Faith, there is no more to be said: but for my part I am not prepared to take up that position.

iv. By importing and using and supplying to the natives buildings and ornaments which they cannot procure for themselves, we tend to pauperize the converts. They cannot supply what they think to be needful, and so they learn to accept the position of passive recipients. By supplying what they cannot supply we check them in the proper impulse to supply what they can supply. Foreign subsidies produce abroad all the ill effects of endowments at home, with the additional disadvantage that they are foreign. The converts learn to rely upon them instead of making every effort to supply their own needs.

v. It is often said that these financial bonds help to maintain unity. Native congregations have before now been held to their allegiance by threats of the withdrawal of pecuniary support. But unity so maintained, by an external bond, is not Christian unity at all. It is simply submission to bondage for the sake of secular advantage and it will fail the moment that any other and stronger motive urges in the direction of separation. There is all the difference in the world between gifts freely made by members of the one body one to another, as manifestations of the spirit of mutual charity which moves in them, and gifts or subsidies made with the intention of checking freedom of action on the part of the recipients. Spiritual forces are more powerful than external bonds, and external bonds never have preserved, and never will preserve, unity. The only unity which is worth preserving is the unity of the Spirit.

vi. By the establishment of great institutions, the provision of large parsonages, mission houses, churches, and all the accompaniments of these things, we tie our missionaries to one place. They cease to be movable evangelists and become pastors. From time to time they go out on tour, but their stations are their chief care, and to their stations they are tied. Even if they find that the station is not well chosen, so much money is invested in it that they cannot easily move. Even if some new opening of larger importance is before them they cannot enter into it without serious and difficult financial adjustments.

vii. Further, these establishments make it very difficult for any native to succeed to the place of a European missionary. The Christians gathered round the station are very conscious of the advantage of having a European in their midst. He has influence with governors, merchants, masters. He can give valuable recommendations. He can return home and plead for his people with societies and charitably-disposed individuals. He can collect money for his schools and hospitals. In time of need and stress he can afford to expend much. He is, or is supposed to be, above the common temptations of the people. He is naturally free from local entanglements. He cannot be accused of seeking to make places for his relations. His judgment is impartial, his opinion unbiased by any divisions or jealousies of local society. All these things incline the native converts to prefer a European to a native as the Head of their station. Consequently, it is very difficult for any native to succeed

57

him. The native has none of these advantages. He cannot tap the sources of supply, he cannot exercise the same charitable liberality, he cannot expect, as a right, the same confidence. He is liable to attack from all sides. He has not even the prestige which attaches to a white face. His position is well-nigh impossible. Moreover, if a native is put in charge of a station, he naturally expects to be paid at the same rate as his white predecessor. If he is not so paid, he feels aggrieved. It is useless to explain to him that a native ought to be able to make one rupee or one dollar go as far as six or seven in the hands of a European. To him the salary for this work, this post, has been fixed at so much, and if he occupies the post he should receive so much. But native Christians, left to themselves, would never have created such a post, and sooner or later they will abolish it. They are accustomed to other standards, and other methods of payment, or support, for teachers. Thus by the establishment of these posts we are creating serious difficulties. We say that we hope the day is not far off when natives will succeed to our places and carry on the work which we have begun. But by the creation of these stations we have put off that day.

From this point of view it is plain that the creation of mission stations with large parsonages and churches is a far more serious difficulty than the establishment of large schools and hospitals. Great colleges and hospitals can more easily be treated as extra-parochial. They are not bound up with the ordinary life of the church. Church life can go on without them, or beside them; and special arrangements made for them do not so nearly touch the community. There must be difficulties with these; but the difficulties connected with parsonages and churches, e.g. in India and the Far East, are already pressing.

viii. Finally, these endowments will sooner or later become a source of fresh difficulties. These buildings, etc., are legally held by foreign missionary societies, which have their headquarters in foreign countries. Sooner or later the native church will grow strong and will insist on managing its own affairs. Are there then to be in the future foreign patronage boards holding buildings in trust, and appointing to posts in the dioceses of native bishops in the territories of independent States? Some of the foreign missionary societies could, and no doubt would, hand over the buildings and patronage to the native church, but others could not, and would not, do that, because they hold the property for the propagation of the peculiar views held by their subscribers at home, and the trustees at home could not be sure that the native bishops would continue to hold those peculiar views whether of doctrine or ritual. Yet it is scarcely conceivable that native churches will tolerate the interference of foreign patronage boards, and a grievous strife may arise over the endowments and the buildings. Of all sources of strife, material possessions are the most prolific. If there have been in the past difficulties between the committees of missionary societies at home and bishops and other leaders in the field, whilst those bishops and leaders were of the same race and speech and habit of thought as the members of the committees, how much more are we to fear difficulties when the bishops and other leaders are natives of independent States. We speak much of the establishment of independent native churches; but the increase of endowments may not prove to be the best means of attaining that end in the future, any more than it has proved to be the best means of attaining it in the past.

(3) Thirdly, St Paul observed the rule that every church should administer its own funds. He certainly never administered any local funds himself. He did indeed bear the offering of the church in Antioch to Jerusalem in the time of the famine; he also, with others, carried the collection of the Four Provinces to Jerusalem. But in the first instance he was acting as the minister of a church on a business for which he had been specially appointed by the Church under the direction of those in authority. In the second, it is extraordinary what pains he took to make it clear that he was acting simply as the messenger of the churches, and even so he did not take the responsibility of administering their charity without associating with himself representatives of all the provinces which contributed to the fund, and taking every possible precaution to ensure that his action should not be misunderstood. In both cases, moreover, he was carrying funds collected by the churches for charitable purposes in a distant place. He certainly did not receive and administer any funds within their own borders. The whole argument of 2 Corinthians 11. 8–14, and 12. 14–18, would have broken down if he had been in the habit of so doing.

With us, today, a very different rule obtains. As soon as a congregation is established, collections are made, and some at least of the money so obtained is sent to the diocesan or district fund. It is taken out of the place in which it is collected under the direction, if not in the hands, of the foreigner. If money is collected for local uses, it is administered under the direction of the foreigner who feels himself responsible for its proper expenditure, and requires a most careful account of it, and himself renders an account of its use to his society at home. In other words, the responsibility for the administration of funds rests upon the shoulders not of the local church but upon the stranger. Is it possible for human ingenuity to devise a scheme better calculated to check the free flow of native liberality, to create misunderstandings, to undermine the independence of the church, and to accentuate racial distinctions?

This modern practice is based partly upon our distrust of native honesty and partly upon our fear of congregationalism. But our distrust of native honesty ought not to exist, and has nothing to do with the case. If the natives administer their own funds, it is their own funds that they administer. They will administer them in their own way, and they will be responsible for the administration to those who supplied them. That they are capable of administering public money the existence of guilds and societies for mutual benefit is proof. They may not administer it at all to our satisfaction, but I fail to see what our satisfaction has to do with the matter. It is not our business. By making it our business we merely deprive our converts of one of the very best educational experiences, and break down one of the most powerful agencies for creating a sense of mutual responsibility. We also load ourselves with a vast burden which we are ill able, and often ill fitted, to bear.

Our fear of congregationalism[1] is really terror of a bugbear. We have had no experience of congregationalism except at home, and there is no reason to suppose that the peculiar motives which lead to congregationalism in England would operate anywhere else. Our fear of congregationalism is, I shrink from saying it, only another name for our fear of independence. We think it quite impossible that a native church should be able to exist without the paternal care of an English overseer. If it were financially independent it might be tempted to dispense with his services, and then, we are persuaded, it would at once fall into every error of doctrine and practice.

---

[1] By 'congregationalism' I mean, of course, not the denomination so-called, but the claim of individual congregations to act as if they were alone in the world, independently of all other Christians.

The congregationalism that we dread is the form of congregationalism which we know in England. The evils of that have bred in us a terrible fear of the very mention of congregational responsibility. Our experience at home has not taught us to dread the suspicion of peculation. We take with us from the West the fear of the one and the ignorance of the other, and we suppose that the danger which arises from each is the same abroad as it is at home. Even at home suspicion of clerical finance exists amongst the laity to a far larger extent than we sometimes imagine, and it were well if our clergy took greater pains to avoid it. But the fact remains that we do not really fear it, whilst we do fear the slightest taint of congregationalism. St Paul's attitude to these two dangers was the exact opposite of ours. He was more afraid of a suspicion of false-dealing than he was of congregationalism. Perhaps in dealing with newly converted people his judgment on the relative danger of the two evils was more sound than ours. Perhaps in dealing with Eastern people we should do well to follow his example.

Note.—There are exceptions to the state of affairs described in this chapter, some important exceptions. Nevertheless, the general practice is, I believe, that which I have described.

CHAPTER 7

The Substance of St Paul's Preaching

Of St Paul's preaching we have in the Acts three examples, the sermon at Antioch in Pisidia (Acts 13. 16–41), the speech at Lystra (Acts 14. 15–17), and the speech at Athens (Acts 17. 22–31). We have also five incidental references to its substance: a description given by the soothsaying girl at Philippi (Acts 16. 17), a summary of his teaching in the synagogue at Thessalonica (Acts 17. 2, 3), a note of the points which struck the Athenians in the Agora as strange (Acts 17. 18), an assertion with reference to its tone and character made by the Town Clerk at Ephesus (Acts 19. 37), and a reiteration of its fundamental elements by St Paul himself in his last address to the Ephesian elders (Acts 20. 21). Besides these, we have an account of his preaching at Corinth given by St Paul himself in his first Epistle to that Church (1 Cor. 2. 2). These accounts are naturally divided into two classes: the preaching in the synagogue, and the preaching to the Gentiles.

The account given by St Luke of the preaching in the synagogue at Thessalonica[1] exactly agrees with, and naturally recalls, the sermon in the synagogue at Antioch, of which the main outline is set before us at some length, and it is unquestioned that that sermon so set forth is, and is intended to be, a type of all St Paul's teaching in the many synagogues to which he went.

The sermon is divided into three parts by dramatic appeals to the attention of his hearers. In the first, St Paul builds upon the past history of the Jewish race and shows that his Gospel is rooted there, that in his message there is no casting away of the things familiar, no denial of the truth of the old revelation made to the Fathers; but rather that the whole history of Israel is the divinely ordered preparation for the new revelation in the Messiah. In the second, he sets forth the facts of the coming and rejection of Jesus and His

[1] Acts 17. 2, 3.

consequent crucifixion. Here it is startling with what simple and unhesitating directness St Paul faces at once this great difficulty, the difficulty which has at all times everywhere been the most serious hindrance in the way of the acceptance of the Gospel—the rejection of the missionary's message by his own people. He does not shrink from it, he does not apologize for it, he does not attempt to conceal its weight. He sets it forth definitely, clearly, boldly; he makes it part of his argument for the truth of his message. It is the fulfilment of prophecy. Then he produces his conclusive proof, the Resurrection, witnessed by the apostles, foretold by the prophets, the fulfilment of the promise. In the third part, he proclaims his message of pardon for all who will receive it, and utters a solemn warning of the consequences which will follow its rejection.

We may see here five elements and four characteristics of St Paul's preaching in the synagogue. The five elements are these:

(1) An appeal to the past, an attempt to win sympathy by a statement of truth common to him and to his hearers. This statement of common belief creates naturally a bond of union. It ensures that the speaker starts with the agreement and approval of his hearers. It also prepares the ground for the new seed. The new truth is shown to grow out of, and to be in harmony with, truth already known and accepted. It does not appear as a strange and startling assertion of something at variance with all that has before guided and enlightened life.

(2) There is a statement of facts, an assertion of things which can be understood, apprehended, accepted, disputed, or proved. There is a presentation of the concrete, tangible, homely story, of something easily grasped, the story of life and death. It is indeed the story of a divine life and a divine death, but it moves on the plane of earth, with which all alike are familiar, the injustice of rulers, the fluctuating passions of crowds, the marvellous recovery, the Divine act of the Resurrection.

(3) There is the answer to the inevitable objection, to the instinctive protest, that all the wisest and most thoughtful and most judicial minds among the speaker's own people have decided against the claims here made. There is a careful presentment of the proof, the evidence of trustworthy men, the agreement of the new truth with the old which has already been acknowledged.

(4) There is the appeal to the spiritual needs of men, to the craving for pardon, and the comforting assurance that in the new teaching may be found peace and confidence.

(5) Finally, there is the grave warning. The rejection of God's message involves serious danger. The way of salvation may be refused, and is commonly refused, but not without peril.

Those are the elements. The characteristics are these: (1) Conciliatoriness and sympathy with the condition of his hearers, readiness to recognize all that is good in them and in their doctrine, sympathy with their difficulties, and care to make the way for them as plain and simple as possible. (2) Courage in the open acknowledgment of difficulties which cannot be avoided, and in the direct assertion of unpalatable truth. There is no attempt to keep the door open by partial statements, no concealment of the real issue and all that it involves, no timid fear of giving offence, no suggestion of possible compromise, no attempt to make things really difficult appear easy. (3) Respect. There is a careful presentation of suitable evidence, there is an appeal to the highest faculties in man. St Paul speaks to men as naturally religious persons, and appeals to them as living souls conscious of spiritual powers and spiritual needs. (4) There is an unhesitating confidence in the truth of his message, and in its power to meet and satisfy the spiritual needs of men.

These four characteristics of St Paul's preaching we shall find everywhere. The elements are not always the same. In particular, there is one element which is very prominent in the preaching to the heathen which has no place here. There is no demand for a break with the old religion. The Jew might become a Christian without abandoning any of the forms of Judaism. A Gentile could not become a Christian without a definite repudiation of his early faith and a definite renunciation of its practice. The break for the Jew was internal only. He ceased to seek his own righteousness in the careful observation of the Law; but outwardly he might still keep the Law. For a Gentile to continue as a Christian to observe the outward forms of his old religion was, to St Paul, impossible. It is also noticeable that there is not here the same insistence upon the imminence of judgment which holds an important place in the preaching to the heathen. The other elements we shall, I think, find more or less prominent in that preaching. With the two exceptions to which I have just alluded, there seems to be a closer agreement between the preaching in the synagogue and the preaching outside than is sometimes allowed.

Of the preaching to the heathen we have two examples given us at some length, the speech at Lystra and the speech at Athens. If these were typical examples of St Paul's preaching to heathen, they would certainly make us think that there was a great gulf between his preaching in the synagogue and his preaching outside. The sermon in the synagogue at Antioch is, comparatively speáking, complete. It contains a real account of the Person and work of the Saviour; the speeches at Lystra and Athens are only preliminary to any teaching about Christ. But as I think we shall see, these are not really typical examples; they are speeches made under exceptional circumstances at dramatic moments in St Paul's career. They are to be compared with 'the Speech on the Stairs'[1] to the crowd in the Temple rather than with the sermon in the synagogue. The speech on the stairs is not a typical example of St Paul's preaching of the Gospel to Jews, neither are these typical examples of St Paul's preaching of the Gospel to Gentiles.

The speech at Lystra is an extremely simple address, designed to check an excited crowd which proposed to do sacrifice to the apostles under the belief that they were gods. It begins with an explanation of the position of the apostles as messengers of God. It contains a simple statement of the nature of God the Creator, and of His personal care for His children, and of the folly of idolatry, with an exhortation to turn from it. Then an answer is given to the natural objection that, if this were true, God would not have left His children so long in ignorance; and proofs are given, drawn from the familiar course of nature, the succession of the seasons, the rain, the harvest.

For all its profundity of tone and philosophic garb, the speech at Athens is singularly like that at Lystra in its actual teaching. Here too St Paul begins with the declaration of the nature of God as Lord of Heaven and earth. Here too he brings out in sharp contrast the contradiction between idolatry and the nature of God; only, in speaking to highly educated men, he tries to draw their sympathy by using quotations from their own literature in support of his argument. Here too he answers the natural objection to his teaching that it is new and that in the past God had left men in ignorance of it. Here too he insists upon the need of repentance. But here he adds, what he has elsewhere specially noted as an important element in his preaching,[2] judgment at hand, with its proof that the Judge has been appointed, and His appointment ratified in the sight of all men by the fact of the Resurrection.

These speeches are chiefly important as illustrations of St Paul's

[1] Acts 22.
[2] Rom. 2. 16.

characteristic method of approach to men and of his wonderful adaptability to changing circumstances. Every one of the characteristics of the sermon at Antioch is here, the sympathy and conciliatory address, the courage, the respect, the confidence; but of the elements very few. There is no setting forth of the Gospel. Professor Ramsay indeed says: 'There is nothing in the reported words of St Paul that is overtly Christian, and nothing (with the possible exception of "the man whom he hath ordained") that several Greek philosophers might not have said.'[1] I cannot quite accept that estimate. There is more, I think, in the last verse of the speech at Athens than Professor Ramsay allows; but Mr Rackham seems to be using equally exaggerated language when in his Commentary on the Acts he describes this speech as 'St Paul's Gospel for the Greeks'.[2] These speeches were rather examples of the way in which St Paul made his first approach to people who were either ignorant of, or in practice denied, the fundamental truths which lie behind the Gospel, than a setting forth of his Gospel. It is important to notice how carefully St Luke calls attention to the meagre results of the preaching in Athens.[3] It is almost certain that the emphasis which St Paul puts upon 'the Cross' in his preaching at Corinth[4] marks, and is meant to mark, a difference between his preaching at Athens and his preaching at Corinth. These speeches then are certainly not representative of St Paul's preaching to the heathen. The few slight references in the Acts to the general tenor of his preaching elsewhere make this abundantly clear. The soothsaying girl at Philippi called attention to two points in St Paul's message, the Most High God, and the Way of Salvation.[5] Now if the first of these is fully represented in the speeches at Athens and Lystra, the second is scarcely referred to in either. Again in St Paul's own summary of his teaching at Ephesus the two elements of the first importance are said to have been, 'Repentance toward God and faith toward our Lord Jesus Christ',[6] and here again if the first finds a place in the speeches at Athens and Lystra, the second finds none. Or, again, the charge made against St Paul at Thessalonica was that he was preaching the

[1] *St Paul the Traveller*, p. 150.
[2] p. 312.
[3] Acts 17. 32–4.
[4] 1 Cor. 2. 2.
[5] Acts 16. 17.
[6] Acts 20. 21.

Kingdom of Christ, 'that there is another King, one Jesus'.[1] But of this there is not a hint in the speeches.

In the light of these facts, it is, I think, impossible to maintain that the speeches at Lystra and Athens represent St Paul's Gospel. It also seems unfair to base upon them a theory that St Paul approached his Gentile hearers with great caution and economy, leading them gradually on from heathenism by a semi-pagan philosophy to Christianity. It is perfectly just to argue from them that the Christian missionary should strive to possess a sound knowledge of the religion of those to whom he speaks, and should approach them with sympathetic understanding of their intellectual position; but that is a totally different thing. It is one thing to preach Christ with a sympathetic knowledge of the belief of those to whom we preach and to base our appeal on the common truth which we hold together with our hearers; it is another thing to spend our time philosophizing when we might be preaching Christ. If St Paul philosophized at Athens he did not philosophize as a general rule, and he has told us quite plainly what he thought was more important. Philosophical disquisitions have no doubt their place; but for mission preaching the supreme subject is 'the Cross', 'Repentance, and Faith'.

It may be justly argued from these speeches that St Paul did not, and that the Christian missionary today should not, make bitter and virulent attacks upon the objects of his hearers' veneration. It is true that St Paul denounced idolatry in strong terms, speaking of 'these vain things'[2] and 'this ignorance',[3] but in doing this he was only taking a position sanctioned by the highest intellects of his day, and recognized by all as a common attitude amongst thoughtful men. Similarly today a missionary in China might denounce in strong terms the folly of Taoist superstitions, and in doing so he would receive the approval of all right-minded Chinese, because that is the proper attitude for an enlightened teacher to take up; it is the attitude of the Sacred Edict. But that is not the same thing as to rail upon the religion of those whom he addresses. St Paul did not do that either at Lystra or at Athens, and the Town Clerk at Ephesus is witness that he did not blaspheme the goddess of that city. This is quite in harmony with the characteristic attitude of St Paul to his

[1] Acts. 17. 7.
[2] Acts 14. 15.
[3] Acts 17. 30.

hearers which I have before noted. Christians in later days, accustomed to more bitter methods of controversy, could not understand this. To St Chrysostom it seemed incredible that St Paul should have refrained from fierce denunciation of the false goddess. He explained the matter by saying that the Town Clerk was not stating a known fact, but simply using a form of speech which he thought calculated to quiet an excited crowd. In later ages this same habit of mind still lingered on, and it is only now dying out. Now, it is happily rare to hear a missionary revile the religion of other people, or hold up the objects of their veneration to scorn and ridicule, and it is to be hoped that it may soon cease altogether.

If we cannot accept the speeches at Athens and Lystra as typical of St Paul's address to heathen people, still we are not left wholly to the guidance of the few scattered statements concerning his main doctrines which I have quoted above. We have as a witness the epistles to the Thessalonians. The first epistle was written about a year after St Paul's first preaching in the city, where, according to Professor Ramsay's calculation he had laboured for only five months. Thus his stay had not been long enough for him to do more than teach the fundamental truths which seemed to him of the first importance; all the circumstances of his visit were still fresh in his memory and he was recalling to the minds of his readers what he had taught them by word of mouth. Now in that epistle[1] we get an extraordinarily clear and coherent scheme of simple mission-preaching not only implied but definitely expressed. Briefly that teaching contains the following elements:

(1) There is one living and true God (1. 9); (2) Idolatry is sinful and must be forsaken (1. 9); (3) The wrath of God is ready to be revealed against the heathen for their impurity (4. 6), and against the Jews for their rejection of Christ and their opposition to the Gospel (2. 15, 16); (4) The judgment will come suddenly and unexpectedly (5. 2, 3); (5) Jesus the Son of God (1. 10), given over to death (5. 10), raised from the dead (4. 14), is the Saviour from the wrath of God (1. 10); (6) The Kingdom of Jesus is now set up and all men are invited to enter it (2. 12); (7) Those who believe and turn to God are now expecting the coming of the Saviour who will return from heaven to receive them (1. 10; 4. 15–17); (8) Meanwhile their life must be pure (4. 1–8), useful (4. 11, 12), and watchful (5. 4–8); (9) To that end God has given them His Holy Spirit (4. 8; 5. 19).[2]

[1] Ramsay, *St Paul the Traveller*, p. 146.
[2] See Lock on First Epistle to the Thessalonians in Hastings' *Dictionary of the Bible*.

This Gospel accords perfectly with the account which St Paul gives of his preaching in his last address to the Ephesian elders,[1] and it contains all the elements which are to be found in all the sermons and in all the notices of St Paul's preaching in the Acts, except only the answers to the objections against the Gospel, and the proofs of its truth which would be manifestly out of place in writing to Christians. The nature of God, one, living, personal, loving; the facts of the life of Jesus Christ, the Son of God, the death, the resurrection: their meaning and their power to supply the spiritual needs of men; the folly of idolatry; the way of salvation: repentance and faith; the doctrine of the kingdom; the nearness of judgment: all are there, not one is omitted, and they form one connected whole of extraordinary power.

We can easily understand how such a Gospel would appeal to the minds of St Paul's hearers. To those who, among the conflicting claims and confused teachings of polytheism, were seeking for some unity in the world of nature and of thought, St Paul brought a doctrine, at once simple and profound, of one personal God living and true, the Creator of all. To men who sought for some intelligent account of the world, its nature and its end, St Paul revealed a moral purpose in the light of which all the perplexities, uncertainties, and apparent contradictions, resolved themselves into a divine harmony. To men of high moral instincts, appalled and dismayed at the impurity of society around them, St Paul offered the assurance of a moral judgment. To men oppressed by the sense of sin he brought the assurance of pardon and release. To the downtrodden, the sad, the hopeless, he opened the door into a kingdom of light and liberty. To those who were terrified by the fear of malignant spirits he revealed a Spirit benignant, watchful and ever present, all-powerful and able at a word to banish the power of darkness. To men dissatisfied with the worship of idols he taught the pure service of one true God. To people whose imaginations were overwhelmed by the terrors and darkness of the grave he gave the assurance of a future beyond the grave in the bliss and peace of the Risen Lord. To the weak who needed support, to sinners bound with the chain of vice, to people unable to cope with the depressed morality of their heathen surroundings, he brought the promise of an indwelling Spirit of power. To the lonely he offered the friendly warmth and society of a

[1] Acts 20. 21.

company all eagerly looking forward to a bright day when Grace would come and this world with all its perplexities and troubles pass away. It is no wonder then that this Gospel of St Paul appealed to men, fired their imaginations, filled them with hope, and strengthened them with power to face persecution.

Yet to embrace this new religion was not easy. There was, as we have seen, in St Paul's preaching a conciliatory, sympathetic attitude towards the heathen. There was no violent attack, no crude and brutal assault upon their beliefs, still less was there any scornful or flippant mocking of their errors. But, on the other hand, there was no weak condoning of the offence of idolatry, no eager anxiety to make the best of a false religion, no hazy suggestion that every religion, if only it is rightly understood, is a worship of the true God and a teaching which leads to Him. St Paul gave his hearers a perfectly clear, definite understanding of what was required of them. To enjoy the hope set before them they must be prepared for a complete break with the past. There was no easy road to Christ's glory, no making the best of both worlds, no hope of salvation but in Christ, and no entrance into the Church except with the certainty of suffering persecution.

There is today a tendency to avoid this stern doctrine. We are tempted rather to exaggerate the truth and virtue of heathen religions, and to minimize the gulf which separates the man who is 'in Christ' from the man who is not. We hesitate to speak, we scarcely dare to think, of idolatry as sin. We have lost the sense that the Judge is at the door and that the wrath of God against all ungodliness is ready to be revealed. We no longer look upon the acceptance of our message as 'deliverance from the wrath to come'. We tend to think that the duty of the Church is rather to Christianize the world than to gather out of the world the elect of God into the fellowship of His Son. We hear men speak vaguely of the salvation of the race rather than of the salvation of the saints.

This attitude of mind is most clearly and amply expressed by Mr Bernard Lucas in *The Empire of Christ*,[1] and it leads him to the conclusion that we ought to receive the Hindu 'without demanding that exclusion from his social environment which baptism and the renunciation of caste involve'. If we begin by insisting that the leavening of the heathen world with Christian ideas is the true aim

[1] Chap. 5.

of the Christian Church, and then argue that the truly appalling character of the complete break with the heathen past—which is involved in the open acceptance of Christianity, and the confession of Christ, and admission into His body—is a stumbling-block in the way of the general acceptance of Christian ideas by pagan nations, we speedily arrive at the conclusion that everything which accentuates the difficulty, or attracts attention to the gravity of the change involved in passing from the one dominion to the other, should be abandoned. If our hope is to see gradual transformation of native religious thought and practice, and the gradual evolution of a higher type, we naturally deprecate sudden and startling rupture. The work of the Christian missionary is not to call men from the heathen temple into the Church of God but to trim the dimly glowing lamp of God in the heathen temple, and to pour into it a few drops of the oil of Christian doctrine till it shines with a new radiance.

Where this tendency manifests itself, it is due to the fact that we have lost the true conception of the nature and work of faith as preached by St Paul. As he taught, the one essential condition of life was faith in our Lord Jesus Christ. But faith in Jesus Christ involved, in itself, a breach with the past. Faith was not a mere intellectual assent to a new theory of religion which could be held whilst the life remained what it was before. It was not a mere acknowledgment of a new moral law, of a duty of following the example of a new Teacher which could be obeyed without breaking away from the old law. It was not a mere recognition of the beauty of the life and teaching of the Lord which might make a man love His character from a distance. It was an act by which a man came into personal contact with the Divine source of life. It was an act by which he opened his soul to the influence of a Spirit. It admitted to a vital union. It was the condition of a new birth. It resulted in a new creation. The moment a man had faith, life for him consisted in union with Christ. Consequently it meant the acceptance of a new source of life. It meant dependence upon Christ for the supply and maintenance of life. It meant the abandonment of the old conception of life, nay, of the very life itself as he before knew it. It meant the casting away of all the former things.

But this total and entire conversion of the inner man, this absolute doing away of the old and acceptance of the new life, being in its nature a real breach and not a formal one, necessarily involved a corresponding outward breach with the old form of life. Of this breach baptism was the sacrament. In baptism the change was effected and realized in fact. Baptism was not a mere formal external act, a symbol of a spiritual fact which was already complete without it. A spiritual conversion which was not also a conversion of life was no conversion at all, but a delusion. Spiritual facts being more real than outward facts must dominate the outward life; or else we are reduced to drawing a sharp line of demarcation between the spiritual and the material worlds and treating them as independent spheres, and that St Paul always refused to do. With the heart man believes, with the mouth he confesses; but a mouth which does not confess disproves the existence of a heart that believes. The soul cannot be God's and the life not God's at the same time. The soul cannot be recreated and the life remain unchanged. The spiritual breach is proved and realized and completed in the outward breach. Where there is no outward change it is safe to deny an inward change. Faith without baptism and all that baptism involved was consequently no part of St Paul's teaching.

Furthermore, this easy doctrine of evangelization has been made more easy for us by the fact that we have lost, in these days, two of the most prominent elements of St Paul's Gospel: the doctrine of judgment at hand, and the doctrine of the wrath of God. St Paul did not preach that in times past men had lived under the stern dominion of law and that with the Gospel had come a day of toleration; he preached that in times past God had been long-suffering, and that now He called upon all men everywhere to repent, because the day of judgment was at hand. He did not preach that the mission of the Gospel was to reveal the true beauty of heathen religions; but that it was to open a door of salvation to those who would flee from the wrath to come. He did not deny the salvation of good heathen; but he did not preach that men could be as certainly saved by being good heathen as by being good Christians. He proclaimed that the man who was 'in Christ' was 'in the way of salvation' 'saved', and the man who was not in Christ was 'perishing'. He did not argue that it was desirable to embroider or conceal the doctrine of the Cross which was a stumbling-block to Jews and Gentiles alike, but that the first duty of him who would find salvation in Christ was to embrace the Cross in baptism and, dying to his heathen past, rise into a new life with Christ.[1] He did not minimize the breach between Christianity and heathenism: he declared that the one was the kingdom of evil, the other the Kingdom of God, and that his work was to turn men 'from darkness to light and from the power of Satan unto God'.

Personally, I feel inclined to believe that in both these respects our modern doctrine is not more true than the doctrine of the ancients, whilst it is far less effective. I believe that in concentrating our thought upon the continuity and uniformity of the world processes we have lost sight of the equally true facts of change, catastrophe, judgment. If there is no judgment 'human life is the only process that we know that comes to no vivid conclusion; moral discipline is the only seed that has no harvest'. There is in St Paul's definite soul-stirring assertion of the wrath of God and the reality of judgment at hand, a truth more profound than any that underlies our somewhat enfeebled ideas of universal benevolence and the determined progress of the race. There is something more true in his denunciation of idolatry as sin than in our denial that it is possible for a man to worship an idol, or in our suggestion that all idolatry is only a road to spiritual worship of the one true God. There is something stronger and better in his unhesitating insistence on the necessity of those who come to Christ breaking with their past than in Mr Bernard Lucas's doctrine that in the Christianizing of the world all men will be brought to Christ. One day I think we shall return to these stern doctrines, realizing in them a truth more profound than we now know; and then we shall preach them with conviction, and being convinced ourselves we shall convince others. 'Knowing the terror of the Lord' we shall persuade men, to the great advancement

[1] Here and elsewhere I use the word 'baptism' in its full sense. When I speak of a man named 'John', I do not mean a corpse or a disembodied spirit, I mean a composite whole, a body which I can see, and a spirit of which I know nothing except what I infer from the appearance of the body. Similarly, when I speak of 'baptism' I do not mean a mere form. I mean a composite whole, a form which I can see and a spirit which gives it meaning and force. If there had been no repentance and faith there would have been no baptism, and if there had been no gift of the Holy Ghost, still less would there have been any baptism. By baptism then, I mean, not only washing, but repentance and faith and Grace of the Holy Ghost and Washing; when I speak of baptism I wish to be understood as speaking of all these, not merely together but in one unity, just as when I speak of 'John' I speak of body and spirit as one unity. That is how I understood St Paul to use the word, e.g. Rom. 6. 3, 4; 1 Cor. 12. 13; Col. 2. 12-20.

of the Kingdom of God. Meanwhile, if only we could avoid explaining away those passages of Holy Scripture which speak of the Second Coming and the Judgment, which we confessedly cannot explain, I believe we should often find that our converts would understand them better than we do and would help us to understand them.

St Paul expected his hearers to be moved. He so believed in his preaching that he knew that it was 'the power of God unto salvation'. This expectation is a very real part of the presentation of the Gospel. It is a form of faith. A mere preaching which is not accompanied by the expectation of faith, is not a true preaching of the Gospel, because faith is a part of the Gospel. Simply to scatter the seed, with a sort of vague hope that some of it may come up somewhere, is not preaching the Gospel. It is indeed a misrepresentation of the Gospel. To preach the Gospel requires that the preacher should believe that he is sent to those whom he is addressing at the moment, because God has among them those whom He is at the moment calling: it requires that the speaker should expect a response. The air of expectation pervades all the accounts of St Paul's preaching. Everywhere we are made to recognize, not only that St Paul expected to make converts, but that others expected it also. This accounts for the opposition which his preaching created. People were afraid of his preaching, and fear is a form of expectation: it is a form of faith. St Paul himself was inspired with the faith of hope: he inspired others with the faith of fear. Everywhere he was surrounded by an atmosphere of faith.

Further, he always contrived to bring his hearers to a point. There was none of the indeterminate, inconclusive talking, which we are apt to describe as 'sowing the seed'. Our idea of 'sowing the seed' seems to be rather like scattering wheat out of a balloon. We read, in our reports, of missionaries on evangelistic tours visiting village after village, talking to little crowds of hearers, telling them the good news; but very little seems to be expected to come of it. Occasionally, of course, grains of wheat scattered out of a balloon will fall upon ploughed and fertile land and will spring up and bear fruit; but it is a casual method of sowing. St Paul did not scatter seeds, he planted. He so dealt with his hearers that he brought them speedily and directly to a point of decision, and then he demanded of them that they should make a choice and act on their choice. In this way he kept the moral issue clearly before them, and made them realize that his preaching was not merely a novel and interesting doctrine, but a life.

The possibility of rejection was ever present. St Paul did not establish himself in a place and go on preaching for years to men who refused to act on his teaching. When once he had brought them to a point where decision was clear, he demanded that they should make their choice. If they rejected him, he rejected them. The 'shaking of the lap',[1] the 'shaking of the dust from the feet',[2] the refusal to teach those who refused to act on the teaching, was a vital part of the Pauline presentation of the Gospel. He did not simply 'go away', he openly rejected those who showed themselves unworthy of his teaching. It was part of the Gospel that men might 'judge themselves unworthy of eternal life'. It is a question which needs serious consideration whether the Gospel can be truly presented if this element is left out. Can there be a true teaching which does not involve the refusal to go on teaching? The teaching of the Gospel is not a mere intellectual instruction: it is a moral process, and involves a moral response. If then we go on teaching where that moral response is refused, we cease to preach the Gospel; we make the teaching a mere education of the intellect. This is why so much of our teaching of the Gospel in schools and zenanas is ineffective. We teach, but we do not teach morally. We do not demand moral response. We are afraid to take the responsibility which morally rests upon us of shaking the lap. We should refuse to give intellectual teaching to a pupil if he refused to give us his attention: we might equally refuse to give religious teaching to a pupil who refused to give us religious attention.

It is a question which needs serious consideration whether we ought to plant ourselves in a town or village and continue for years teaching people who deliberately refuse to give us a moral hearing. We persevere in this in spite of the fact that near at hand are men who are eager and willing to give us that moral hearing. We are afraid to take the responsibility which morally rests upon us of shaking the lap. We have forgotten that the same Lord who gave us the command to go, gave us the command to shake off the dust from our feet. We have lost the art of shaking the lap, we have learnt the

[1] Acts 18. 6.
[2] St Matt. 10. 14.

75

art of steeling our hearts and shutting up the bowels of our com-
passion against those who cry to us for the Gospel.

There is one other aspect of St Paul's preaching which is often
taken for granted, but is certainly not true—that the Gospel of St
Paul was purely individualistic. To the heathen crowd St Paul
addressed himself as to a mass of souls from amongst which he was to
gather the elect children of God. But he did not approach them as an
isolated prophet: he came as an Apostle of the Church of God, and
he did not simply seek to gather out individual souls from amongst
the heathen, he gathered them into the society of which he was a
member. He did not teach them that they would find salvation by
themselves alone, but that they would find it in the perfecting of the
Body of Christ. Souls were not invited to enter into an isolated
solitary religious life of communion with Christ: they were invited to
enter the society in which the Spirit manifested Himself and in which
they would share in the communication of His life. It was incon-
ceivable that a Christian taught by St Paul could think of himself as
obtaining a personal salvation by himself. He became one of the
brethren. He shared in the common sacraments. The Church was not
an invisible body formed of unknown 'believers'. Men were admitted
by their baptism into a very visible society, liable to be attacked by
very visible foes. The Apostle who preached to them was a member
of it, and he preached as a member of it, and as a member of it he
invited them to enter it, to share its privileges and its burdens, its
glory and its shame. Entrance into it was guarded by a very definite
and unmistakable sacrament.[1] Thus Christianity was from the very
beginning both individualistic and socialistic.

St Paul's preaching ever appealed to and demanded the exercise
of the two highest and deepest convictions of men, their sense of
individual responsibility and their sense of social communion with
their fellows. Repentance and faith are the keynotes of his preaching.
He strove always to bring men to make that act of spiritual surrender
by which they renounce the past and turn to Christ. In repentance
they confess their past wrongdoing; in faith they find forgiveness as
members of Christ's Body. In repentance they recognize their weakness; in faith they find strength by the administration of the Spirit of

---

[1] 'Christian life properly began with baptism. . . . Till that decisive step was
taken, he could not be more than a friendly heathen.'—Gwatkin. *Early Eccl.
Hist.*, i, 247.

Christ. In repentance they confess the way in which they have walked is a way of death; in faith they find in the Kingdom of Christ the way of life. In repentance they break with a sinful world; in faith they enter the Church.

PART III

The Training of Converts

The Teaching

From what has already been said it is manifest that St Paul did not go about as a missionary preacher merely to convert individuals: he went to establish churches from which the light might radiate throughout the whole country round. The secret of success in this work lies in beginning at the very beginning. It is the training of the first converts which sets the type for the future. If the first converts are taught to depend upon the missionary, if all work, evangelistic, educational, social is concentrated in his hands, the infant community learns to rest passively upon the man from whom they receive their first insight into the Gospel. Their faith having no sphere for its growth and development lies dormant. A tradition very rapidly grows up that nothing can be done without the authority and guidance of the missionary, the people wait for him to move, and, the longer they do so, the more incapable they become of any independent action. Thus the leader is confirmed in the habit of gathering all authority into his own hands, and of despising the powers of his people, until he makes their inactivity an excuse for denying their capacity. The fatal mistake has been made of teaching the converts to rely upon the wrong source of strength. Instead of seeking it in the working of the Holy Spirit in themselves, they seek it in the missionary. They put him in the place of Christ, they depend upon him.

In allowing them, or encouraging them, to do this, the missionary not only checks the spiritual growth of his converts and teaches them to rely upon a wrong source of strength; he actually robs them of the strength which they naturally possess and would naturally use. The more independent spirits amongst them can find no opportunity for exercising their gifts. All authority is concentrated in the hands of the missionary. If a native Christian feels any capacity for Christian work, he can only use his capacity under the direction, and in accordance with the wishes, of that supreme authority. He can do little in his own way; that is, in the way which is natural to him. Consequently, if he is to do any spiritual work he must either so suppress himself as to act in an unnatural way, or he must find outside the Church the opportunity which is denied to him within her borders, or he must put aside the desire which God has implanted in his soul to do spiritual work for Christ, and content himself with secular employment.[1] If he does the first, he works all his life as a cripple: if he takes either of the two other courses, the Church is robbed of his help. It is almost impossible to imagine that a native 'prophet' could remain within the church system as it exists in many districts. If a prophet arose he would either have all the spirit crushed out of him, or he would secede. The native Christian ministers who remain are those who fall into lifeless submission to authority, or else spend their lives in discontented misery, feeling that they have lost themselves not to God but to a foreign system. Thus the community is robbed of its strength: its own forces are weakened whilst it depends upon the most uncertain of props and the most unnatural. In the result the missionary is left to deplore the sad condition of a Christian church which seems in danger of falling away the moment he leaves it.

If there is a striking difference between St Paul's preaching and ours there is a still greater difference between his method of dealing with his converts and that common among us today. Indeed, I think we may say that it is in his dealing with his converts that we come to the heart of the matter and may hope to find one secret of his amazing success. With us today this is the great difficulty. We can gather in converts, we often gather in large numbers; but we cannot train them to maintain their own spiritual life. We cannot establish the church on a self-supporting basis. Our converts often display great virtues, but they remain, too often for generations, dependent upon us. Having gathered a Christian congregation the missionary is too often tied to it and so hindered from further evangelistic work. This difficulty unquestionably arises from our early training of our converts, and therefore it is of supreme importance that we should endeavour to discover, as far as we can, the method of St Paul in training his. For he succeeded exactly where we fail.

[1] 'At Conferences in three of the principal cities, attended by the leading Chinese pastors and Christian teachers, one of the chief reasons given by them to explain why more of the ablest Christian students do not enter the ministry, was the strong feeling of dissatisfaction with the subordinate position held by native pastors' (Dr Mott, *Decisive Hour*, p. 22).

The first and most striking difference between his action and ours is that he founded 'churches' whilst we found 'Missions'. The establishment of Missions is a peculiarity of our modern methods of which I have already pointed out many disadvantages in the chapter on finance. Here it must be added that they have not proved themselves in practice to be very convenient or effective instruments for creating indigenous churches. They are intended to be a means to that end. The theory is that the Mission stands at first in a sort of paternal relationship to the native Christians: then it holds a co-ordinate position side by side with the native organization; finally it ought to disappear and leave the native Christians as a fully-organized church. But the Mission is not the Church. It consists of a missionary, or a number of missionaries, and their paid helpers, supported by a foreign Society. There is thus created a sort of dual organization. On the one hand there is the Mission with its organization; on the other is the body of native Christians, often with an organization of its own. The one is not indeed separate from the other, but in practice they are not identified. The natives always speak of 'the Mission' as something which is not their own. The Mission represents a foreign power, and natives who work under it are servants of a foreign government. It is an evangelistic society, and the natives tend to leave it to do the evangelistic work which properly belongs to them. It is a model, and the natives learn simply to imitate it. It is a wealthy body, and the natives tend to live upon it, and expect it to supply all their needs. Finally, it becomes a rival, and the native Christians feel its presence as an annoyance, and they envy its powers; it becomes an incubus, and they groan under the weight of its domination. In the early stages it maintains a high standard of morality, and in all stages it ministers largely to the advancement of the native community by its educational and medical establishments; but it always keeps the native Christians in check, and its relations with them are difficult and full of perils. A large part of modern books on Missions is concerned with the attempt to justify these relations and to find some way of escape from these difficulties. For St Paul they did not exist, because he did not create them. He set up no organization intermediate between his preaching and the establishment of a fully organized indigenous church. It is interesting to speculate what would have happened, if, at the end of his first missionary journey, St Paul had hastened back to Antioch to entreat for the assistance of two or three presbyters to supervise the growth of the churches in South Galatia, pleading that unless he could secure this help he would be unable to enter the open door which he saw before him; or if instead of ordaining elders he had appointed catechists, keeping the administration of the sacraments in his own hands. From our own experience we can easily guess. But our experience was not his experience, because our practice was not his practice.

The facts are these: St Paul preached in a place for five or six months and then left behind him a church, not indeed free from the need of guidance, but capable of growth and expansion. For example, according to Ramsay, St Paul preached in Lystra for about six months on his first missionary journey, then he ordained elders and left for about eighteen months. After that he visited the church for the second time, but only spent a few months in the province. Then for the last time, after an interval of three years, he visited them again, but again he was only a month or two in the province. From this it is clear that the churches of Galatia were really founded and established in the first visit. The same fact is also clear from the language used in the Acts concerning St Paul's second visit. When he was about to set forth, St Luke says that he proposed to Barnabas to 'go and visit our brethren in every city where we have preached the word of the Lord, and see how they do', and he is described as passing through Galatia delivering the decrees of the Jerusalem Council with the result that 'the churches were established in the faith and increased in number daily'. This is not language which could be used of a missionary visiting congregations which could not stand without his presence, or which lacked any of the fundamentals of settled Christian life: it is language which speaks of organized and established communities. Similarly in Macedonia, Professor Ramsay calculates that St Paul did not stay in Thessalonica more than five months, and he did not visit the place again for over five years, yet he writes to 'the church of the Thessalonians'[1] and speaks of it as being on the same footing as 'the churches of God in Judea'.[2] At Corinth St Paul spent a year and a half at his first visit and then did not go there again for three or four years, but he wrote letters as to a fully equipped and well-established church.

[1] 1 Thess. 1. 1.
[2] 1 Thess. 2. 14.

Now these are typical examples of his work. The question before us is, how he could so train his converts as to be able to leave them after so short a time with any security that they would be able to stand and grow. It seems at first sight almost incredible. In the space of time which amongst us is generally passed in the class of hearers, men were prepared by St Paul for the ministry. How could he prepare men for Holy Orders in so brief a time? How could he even prepare them for holy baptism? What could he have taught them in five or six months? If any one today were to propose to ordain men within six months of their conversion from idolatry, he would be deemed rash to the verge of madness. Yet no one denies that St Paul did it. The sense of stupefaction and amazement that comes over us when we think of it is the measure of the distance which we have travelled from the apostolic method.

We commonly attempt to alleviate the sense of oppression by arguing, first, that his converts were people wholly and totally different from ours, and, then, that as a matter of fact he did not really leave them, because he was constantly in touch with them by messengers and by letters. In this way we escape from the difficulty, but it is only by blinding our eyes. I have already attempted to describe some characteristics of the society from which his converts were taken. It is quite impossible to imagine or believe that they came to St Paul with any special advantages. If we take the highest possible view of the condition of the people at Lystra, or Thessalonica, or Corinth, a few had some acquaintance with the Old Testament, and the requirements of the Jewish Law, a few had some knowledge of Greek Philosophy, the vast majority were steeped in the follies and iniquities of idolatry and were the slaves of the grossest superstitions. Not one knew anything of the life and teaching of the Saviour. In India and China we are constantly in touch with material as good as any to be found at Lystra. Before now we have received high caste, educated men, before now we have received mortal men endowed with profound spiritual capacities, who would compare well with the best of the people with whom St Paul had to deal. Moreover, our converts today possess one advantage of great importance which was denied to his. Today the whole Bible is printed in the vernacular of nearly every people, and in addition there is a considerable and rapidly-growing theological literature. This advantage is so great that, by itself alone, it should make us cautious of arguing that we cannot follow the Pauline method because his converts were in a better position than ours.

Neither is it just to minimize St Paul's work by over-estimating the extent of the supervision exercised by the Apostle over his converts by means of letters and messengers. The only possible case in the Four Provinces, on which can be based an argument to guide and direct the organization of a new church for any length of time, arises out of our ignorance of the movements of St Luke from the time at which he arrived at Philippi with St Paul on his second missionary journey till the time at which St Paul met him there on his third journey. St Luke says that 'we', including himself, arrived at Philippi[1] and that 'they', i.e. St Paul and Silas, left for Thessalonica.[2] Five years later St Paul and his company arrived at Philippi, and the 'we', including St Luke, sailed away to Troas.[3] This has seemed to many a sufficient reason for arguing that St Luke was left at Philippi all that time. In that case he must, without doubt, have been a pillar of strength to the church in that place. If that was really the case, it does not affect the truth of the statement that it was not St Paul's usual practice to establish his fellow-workers as ministers to the infant congregations which he founded. If St Luke stayed at Philippi, it was on his own initiative, either, as Professor Ramsay suggests, because he had a house there, or for some other private reason. It is impossible to argue from an isolated and doubtful incident of this kind against the whole course of St Paul's action elsewhere.

St Paul left Timothy and Silas at Beroea, but only for a very short time, with orders to rejoin him as quickly as possible. He sent Timothy from Athens to Thessalonica. He sent Timothy at least once and Titus two or three times to Corinth. But there is no mention of any messenger being sent to Galatia, and the terms in which these visits of his fellow-workers to Macedonia and Achaia are spoken of, at once reveal the fact that they were not sent to minister to and to educate congregations ignorant of the fundamental truths and incapable of maintaining their own life. St Paul was careful not to lose touch with his new converts. They sorely needed visits and instruction, and they received them. I have no doubt that he was in

[1] Acts 16. 12, 13.
[2] Acts 17. 1.
[3] Acts 20. 6.

constant communication with them by one means or another. But there is an immense difference between dealing with an organized church through letters and messengers and occasional visits, and exercising direct personal government. Visits paid at long intervals, occasional letters, even constant communication by means of deputies, is not at all the same thing as sending catechists or teachers to stay and instruct converts for a generation whilst they depend upon the missionary for the ministration of the sacraments. Nothing can alter or disguise the fact that St Paul did leave behind him at his first visit complete churches. Nothing can alter or disguise the fact that he succeeded in so training his converts that men who came to him absolutely ignorant of the Gospel were able to maintain their position with the help of occasional letters and visits at crises of special difficulty. We want then to consider: (1) What St Paul taught his converts; (2) How he prepared them for baptism and ordination.

(1) I have already tried to set forth the elements of the simple Gospel contained in the public preaching of St Paul. That Gospel involves a doctrine of God the Father, the Creator; a doctrine of Jesus, the Son, the Redeemer, the Saviour; a doctrine of the Holy Spirit, the indwelling source of strength; but these in the simplest and most practical form.

Besides this St Paul left a tradition to which he constantly refers.[1] In the 1st Epistle to the Corinthians this tradition, as touching two points of Christian practice and doctrine, is set forth in some detail. We see there that the teaching on the Holy Communion involved a careful statement of the institution of the rite and of the manner in which it was to be observed;[2] we see that the teaching of the resurrection included an account of the appearances of the Lord to the disciples after His death, beginning with the appearance to St Peter and ending with the appearance to St Paul on the Damascus road.[3] Hence we may conclude that the doctrine involved in the preaching was reinforced, in the tradition delivered to converts, by more or less detailed teaching of the facts in the life of Christ upon which the doctrine rested.

---

[1] 2 Thess. 2. 15; 3. 6; 1 Cor. 11. 2; 11. 23; 1 Tim. 6. 20; 2 Tim. 1. 13; 2. 2; 3. 14; Tit. 1. 9.
[2] 1 Cor. 11. 23–26.
[3] 1 Cor. 15. 3–8.

It is unfortunate that we cannot determine whether this tradition was written down. Professor Harnack tells us that 'the Jews had already drawn up a catechism for proselytes',[1] and any one who has had the slightest experience in the difficulty of teaching heathen converts will at once naturally understand how the need of a book of instruction, which could be left in the hands of the leaders of these early churches, must have pressed upon St Paul. The first work missionaries commonly do, when they approach a new country, is to translate such a book. We should naturally incline to imagine that St Paul would have been compelled by the circumstances of the case to procure a short life of Christ with an appendix on Christian morality.[2] Yet there is no sure ground for arguing that in these early years such a book existed. It is strange that St Paul makes no references in his writings to any parable or miracle of Christ; and references to, or quotations from, His sayings are extraordinarily scanty. On the other hand, references to His death and resurrection abound. We can only suppose then that St Paul relied upon an oral teaching of those fundamental facts.

Further, St Paul accepted and delivered to his converts as an inspired book the Jewish Old Testament. With him began that strange process by which a book, originally the peculiar property of one people, was taken from them and made a foundation stone of the religion of another people; all its references to the original tribe being reinterpreted so as to be applicable to the new people, all its rites spiritualized so as to have a meaning and instruction for a people who did not observe them in the letter; until at last the new people so made the book their own that they denied to the original possessors any part or lot in it. St Paul taught his converts to read the Old Testament and to read it in a mystic sense as applying to Gentile Christians. That does not seem to us easy. We do not as a rule find it easy to teach heathern converts to use the Old Testament properly even when they have the whole of the New Testament with which to illuminate it. It does not seem to us the most convenient of text-books to put into the hands of new converts. We wonder how St Paul could have taught the common people, the slaves, the

---

[1] *Expansion of Christianity*, vol. i, p. 391–2.

[2] I cannot help thinking that critics in attempting to solve the problem of the date of the written gospels have not paid sufficient attention to this urgent practical demand for a written life of the Lord.

labourers, to use such a book in six months, even if they could read at all when they came to him?

St Paul plainly lectured, using the Old Testament as his text-book. The more intelligent speedily caught his method of reading and interpreting it.[1] The meetings of the church were gatherings for mutual instruction. Anyone who had been reading the book and had discovered a passage which seemed to point to Christ, or an exhortation which seemed applicable to the circumstances of their life, or a promise which encouraged him with hope for this life or the next, produced it and explained it for the benefit of all. That was the secret, there lay the source of all the early Christian literature.

That is better than sending a catechist to instruct a congregation. The catechist conducts a service and preaches a sermon: the others listen, or get into the habit of not listening; the local prophet is silent. St Paul did not send catechists to teach. Timothy, Titus, Secundus, Gaius, and the rest, after a short time, left their native congregations and followed St Paul, ready to be sent anywhere with special instruction, or exhortation, or direction, to any congregation which was in a difficulty; but he did not set them over congregations of Christians as catechists are set by us. By this means St Paul was always calling out more and more the capacities of the people in the church. But he might have established Timothy at Lystra or at Thessalonica; in that case, people who, in Timothy's absence, were forced to think and speak, would have remained silent.

Finally, he taught them the form of administration and the meaning of the two sacraments of Baptism and the Lord's Supper. There is not a shadow of evidence to support the notion that these sacraments were considered optional in the early Church. In the writings of St Paul it is taken for granted that every Christian has been baptized and that all meet habitually at the Table of the Lord. To wrest the passage in the First Epistle to the Corinthians[2] into a depreciation of baptism, in the face of the whole teaching of all the other Epistles, is simply to deny the use of words to convey meaning. Further, it is universally taken for granted that those to whom St Paul wrote were familiar with the form of administration of these sacraments and with the essential doctrine implied in them. Thus far St Paul must have taught his first converts himself.

[1] See note on pp. 126, 127.
[2] 1 Cor. 1. 14–17.

Thus St Paul seems to have left his newly-founded churches with a simple system of Gospel teaching, two sacraments, a tradition of the main facts of the death and resurrection, and the Old Testament. There was apparently no form of service, except of course the form of the sacraments, nor any form of prayer, unless indeed he taught the Lord's Prayer.[1] There is no certain evidence of the existence of a written gospel or of a formal creed. This seems to us remarkably little. We can hardly believe that a church could be founded on so slight a basis. And yet it is possible that it was precisely the simplicity and brevity of the teaching which constituted its strength. There is a very grave danger in importing complete systems of worship and theology. We lay great stress on the constant repetition of formal services; we make it our boast that our Prayer Book, year by year in orderly cycle, brings before us the whole system of the faith, and we import that Prayer Book and hand it over to new congregations. But it is too complete. It contains too much. The new converts cannot grasp anything securely. They are forced to go through the whole cycle. Before they have learnt addition they must study division, before they have mastered division they must face fractions and decimals, and then round again and again, until they cease to make any effort to master the truth. By teaching the simplest elements in the simplest form to the many, and by giving them the means by which they could for themselves gain further knowledge, by leaving them to meditate upon these few fundamental truths, and to teach one another what they could discover, St Paul ensured that his converts should really master the most important things. Catechists with Prayer Books cannot take the place of long meditation and private study and united search, and oft-repeated lessons in the simplest and most necessary truth. We are sometimes astonished at the knowledge and zeal of a man who has heard one simple sermon on one Christian doctrine, and has taken home with him one simple book, a gospel, or a catechism. After two, or three, or many years he returns and displays a spiritual insight which astonishes us. He has made his one truth his own, and that illumines the whole of his world, whilst our Prayer-Book-fed Christians often have a smattering of knowledge of all the faith, and yet have little light by which to walk. The Creed is really very simple, and very brief; but it may be made very long and very obscure. A man does not need to know much

[1] See Chase, *The Lord's Prayer in the Early Church.*

to lay hold on Christ. St Paul began with simplicity and brevity.[1]

In doing this he ran grave risks. It is characteristic of St Paul that he had such faith in Christ and in the Holy Spirit indwelling in the Church that he did not shrink from risks. How great those risks were, is illustrated by the Judaistic controversy in Galatia, and by the moral and eucharistic scandals at Corinth. On a most serious point of doctrine, on most important points of practice, two of his churches fell into grievous error.

The first shows how lightly the Galatians were armed with controversial weapons against a class of preachers whom St Paul knew to exist, and with what ease they were misled on one of the most vital points of St Paul's doctrine. The new teaching cut away the very foundation of St Paul's work and the difficulty arose on a question with which St Paul became familiar quite early in his career. Yet his converts fell. It has been argued by Bishop Mylne[2] that this catastrophe was due to the fact that St Paul in his first missionary journey had not yet learnt the necessity of laying a deep foundation, that he had not appreciated the danger of trusting the future of the church to ill-instructed converts.

I do not think that this argument is tenable. There is no sign of repentance in all St Paul's dealings with the Galatians. He visited them again and again, and he wrote them a letter; but there is no suggestion that he regretted that he had too hastily committed the Gospel to their care. On the contrary his letter is full of the most earnest insistence upon the necessity of preserving their freedom. From beginning to end it implies that he desires for them more freedom, not that he regrets that he had given them freedom.

Still less is there any sign in the Acts that St Luke thought St Paul had made a mistake in his practice in his first journey. There is not a hint of any kind that such was his opinion. St Luke sets forth St Paul's journeys as journeys guided by the Holy Ghost to a success-

---

[1] Though I think it unwise to *begin* our teaching to new converts by translating and teaching by heart the creeds as we have them in their present form, yet I am not one of those who hold that we can, or should go 'behind the creeds' and try to preach a 'Christ of the gospels' as opposed to 'the Christ of the creeds'. We may teach simply to simple people, as the Church Catechism teaches an abbreviated explanation of the Apostles' Creed to little children, but behind all our teaching, as behind that abbreviated explanation, there must be the catholic creeds. The moment questions are asked about the meaning of the abbreviated creed, the catholic creeds contain the only answer possible for us.

[2] *Missions to Hindus*, pp. 84, 85.

ful issue; he shows us St Paul using one method everywhere, in Antioch and in Thessalonica, in Lystra and in Corinth; and everywhere alike he shows us the fruit which resulted. There is no suggestion whatever that St Paul made a mistake in committing the future of the churches in Galatia to ill-instructed converts, or that he afterwards saw his error and repented of it.

I have often heard missionaries use the argument of Bishop Mylne to justify their interminable government and instruction of their converts; but the argument is vain unless we are prepared to maintain that St Paul remained all his life quite ignorant of true missionary methods. He stayed, it is true, longer at Corinth than he did in Galatia, but the history of the Corinthian church might equally be used as an argument that he had not learnt the danger of entrusting the future of the church to ill-instructed converts.

At Corinth we find the astonishing fact that the whole church could tolerate the grossest immorality of life and the most disgraceful conduct at the celebration of the Lord's Supper. There is no question that St Paul was horrified. The doctrine of the Lord's Supper was a subject, as he himself declared, of his most careful teaching. In his epistle he recalls to them exactly what he had taught them about it, and says that he himself had received it directly from the Lord. He had been teaching in that church for eighteen months, that is, three times as long as he had taught any of his earlier congregations. During all that time he must frequently have celebrated the Lord's Supper. The Corinthian church was renowned for its learning; it should, therefore, have known best the teaching and practice of the Apostle. Yet we find in that church the most appalling and flagrant violations of his fundamental teaching in the matter of the simplest and most necessary church practice. We should naturally have expected that if St Paul had stayed only a month or two with his converts, if they had learnt anything at all about the Lord's Supper, they would have learnt how to celebrate it. We should naturally have expected that if St Paul had taught them anything at all about morality he would have taught them not to tolerate conduct universally condemned by their heathen neighbours. It is quite certain that if any missionary today established a church in which such flagrant violations of the simplest church rules of practice occurred, we should at once be told that his methods were hopelessly bad. Consequently if the apostasy of the Galatians is a proof that St

Paul on his first missionary journey knew nothing of missionary methods, the failure of the Corinthians in practice will equally prove that he knew nothing of them at the end of his second. Yet the fact remains that he was the most successful founder of churches that the world has ever seen.

Paradoxical as it may seem, I think that it is quite possible that the shortness of his stay may have conduced in no small measure to St Paul's success. There is something in the presence of a great teacher that sometimes tends to prevent smaller men from realizing themselves. They more readily feel their responsibility, they more easily and successfully exert their powers, when they see that, unless they come forward, nothing will be done. By leaving them quickly St Paul gave the local leaders opportunity to take their proper place, and forced the church to realize that it could not depend upon him, but must depend upon its own resources. We have already seen how he did this in all matters of local finance. By retiring early, he did the same thing in matters of government and education.

One other effect of St Paul's training is very clear. His converts became missionaries. It seems strange to us that there should be no exhortations to missionary zeal in the Epistles of St Paul. There is one sentence of approval, 'From you sounded out the word of the Lord',[1] but there is no insistence upon the command of Christ to preach the Gospel. Yet Dr Friedländer is certainly right when he says, 'While the Jews regarded the conversion of unbelievers as, at the most, a meritorious work, for the Christians the spread of the doctrine of salvation was the highest and most sacred duty'.[2] The Christians of the Four Provinces were certainly zealous in propagating the faith, and apparently needed no exhortation on the subject. This surprises us: we are not always accustomed to find our converts so zealous. Yet it is not really surprising. Christians receive the Spirit of Jesus, and the Spirit of Jesus is the missionary spirit, the Spirit of Him who came into the world to bring back lost souls to the Father. Naturally when they receive that Spirit they begin to seek to bring back others, even as He did.

The reason of our failure is, I believe, largely due to the fact that we quench that Spirit. We educate our converts to think, as we, accustomed to a long-established and highly-organized church, naturally

[1] Thess. 1. 8.
[2] *Roman Life and Manners*, iii, 186.

think, that none but duly appointed ministers may preach. We dread the possible mistakes of individual zeal. The result is that our converts hesitate to speak of religion to others. They throw the responsibility upon the licensed evangelist and 'the mission'. They do not feel any responsibility themselves to evangelize the world. Their mouths are closed. Here and there, of course, we find a man so full of the Spirit of the Lord that he cannot hold his peace, but he is a comparatively rare exception.

We need to begin again to teach ourselves and our people what Spirit we are of, and to give liberty that the word of the Lord may have free course. When we do that, the church will again reveal itself in its true character and become self-propagating.

CHAPTER 9

The Training of Candidates for Baptism and Ordination

We have tried to discover what teaching St Paul gave to his converts. This teaching followed, it did not precede, baptism. For baptism, apparently very little knowledge of Christian truth was required as an indispensable condition. St Paul baptized the jailor at Philippi, for instance, upon his bare confession of belief in Jesus as Saviour, after an instruction which only lasted an hour or two in the night. Under such circumstances he certainly could not have taught the man very much of the life and doctrine of Christ.[1] He was satisfied that a spiritual change had taken place; there was some sign of repentance, some profession of faith, and that sufficed. Apparently,

---

[1] We must not, however, lay too great stress upon this. Archdeacon Moule in *Half a Century in China* (pp. 141, 142) tells a very interesting story which illustrates with singular clearness the extraordinary power of the mind of man directed by the Holy Spirit to receive the truth of the Gospel and to grasp in a very short time its main principles. He says that the teacher of a village school happened to pass his preaching room in Hangchow and was attracted by the sign over the door. He inquired for the preacher and was introduced to Mr Tai, the catechist, who for 'two or three hours out of the Law of Moses and the Psalms, the Prophets and the Gospels, expounded to him the things concerning Jesus Christ'. Archdeacon Moule continues, 'Then they came over to the mission house to see me; and as I welcomed this stranger and heard a little of his history, I was astonished to observe how eagerly he brushed aside preliminary topics and went straight to the point, narrating with clearness and earnestness the Gospel story, and discussing Christian doctrine. I asked him politely how long he had been a Christian. "I do not understand you, sir," he said. "I know not what a Christian is." "How long, then," I continued, "have you been acquainted with the Bible and Christian literature, enabling you to speak so clearly on these matters?" "For a period of two hours and a half," he said; "I never heard of Jesus or met with preachers or Christian books till Mr Tai read with me and instructed me." He seemed on the spot to have received the truth of God in the love of it, and after thirty-five years of chequered life he is living still, a headstrong, wayward man, as he has shown himself from time to time, but never abandoning his faith, and possessed of a sort of genius and unquenchable zeal for evangelization.' Here we may find perhaps a striking parallel to the case of the Philippian jailor. Such a man as this I suppose St Paul would have baptized on the spot, with all his household if he had any. It is also noteworthy that Mr Tai was 'a catechist'. He would have been ordained elder by St Paul without any delay if he had been a member of any settled congregation.

any one who was prepared to confess his sins and acknowledge Jesus as Lord might be baptized. This seems to be the inevitable conclusion to be drawn from the account of the baptism of whole households. The head of the house accepted Christ as the Saviour; the household did so too, following their natural leader. They were all alike baptized, and then instructed as members of the Christian congregation.

But it does not follow that the great body of converts were baptized without any careful instruction. We know that very early in the history of the Church a complete system of training was provided. Even if we suppose that many of St Paul's converts were baptized without much teaching, it does not follow that the rite was carelessly and indiscriminately administered.

There is nothing in the evidence before us to show that St Paul would have approved the practice of some who have baptized multitudes of uninstructed people in order to secure that their children might receive a Christian education, with the hope that the second generation would become Christian in thought and deed. There is still less to show that he would have approved of the practice of others who have baptized multitudes of heathen on their own undivided responsibility, simply because they have thought that they had evidence that their words had gone home and that the hearts of the people had been touched, and thereafter have only too often left them, an isolated, unorganized group of individuals, baptized indeed, but wholly ignorant how to walk as becomes the Gospel of Christ.

On the other hand, there is nothing in the evidence before us to support the somewhat stiff practice of many of the Anglican missions where a definite and very long period of probation in the classes of hearers and catechumens is prescribed, and exceptions can only be made with the special permission of the bishop. We have adopted this practice in some form or other, more or less rigid, in order that the reality and sincerity of converts may be thoroughly tested, and that they may receive the fullest possible education in Christian doctrine and morals before they are admitted into the company of the faithful. By this means we have undoubtedly restricted the number of our converts, and it is not certain that we have succeeded in attaining an exceptionally high standard of morals and education. We have also run a great risk of confusing the minds of the converts as to the true meaning and nature of baptism. We have taught them that union with Christ is the source of strength, we have taught them that baptism is the sacrament of unity, and then we have told them that they must prove their sincerity by practising virtue in their own strength before they can be admitted to the sacrament by which they are to receive strength to be virtuous. In other words, we have taught them that the one great need of men is Christ, and that without Christ men cannot attain to righteousness, and then that they must attain to righteousness by themselves in order to receive Christ.

The evidence in the New Testament here, as elsewhere, will not provide us with a neat, ready-made rule, which we can follow without thought. What it does show is that in St Paul's teaching the requirements for holy baptism were repentance and faith. The moment a man showed that he had repentance and faith he was baptized into Christ Jesus, in order that Christ in him might perfect that repentance and faith, and bring it to its full end, holiness in the Body of Christ.

The question of difficulty is, Who is to decide whether the candidate is honest in his confession of repentance and faith?

In some cases it is certain that St Paul himself was the sole judge of the reality of the spiritual change, and of the truth of the profession; but it is equally certain that this was not always the case. The majority of the Christians were baptized in his absence; and even when he was present, he did not always baptize them himself. The saying in the first Epistle to the Corinthians that Christ sent him 'not to baptize, but to preach the Gospel',[1] has surely a wider reference than to that one city. It is a general truth expressed in general terms. I cannot reconcile this statement with the common assertion that St Paul, or his companions in travel, acting on his authority, made it a general practice to baptize all the early converts. Professor Swete, for example, says that it is probable that St Paul's companions generally baptized,[2] and this opinion is commonly taken for granted. But there is really no evidence by which to support it.

In Corinth we know that St Paul baptized only three or four people,[3] one of whom was a man of influence and authority.[4] We

[1] 1 Cor. 1. 17.
[2] *Holy Spirit in New Testament*, p. 107.
[3] 1 Cor. 1. 14, 16.
[4] Acts 18. 8.

know that when a brother was excommunicated, St Paul did not act alone, and that he did not ordain without first obtaining the approval of the brethren. The inference seems to me irresistible that St Paul and his fellow-workers admitted first only a few people of known reputation, who showed unmistakable signs of faith, and thereafter left the duty of accepting or refusing candidates very largely to these men, who were themselves from the very nature of the case in a position to possess or to acquire sound knowledge of the character and motives of those who offered themselves for baptism. But whether he did this whilst he was present or not, it is perfectly certain that his speedy departure threw this responsibility upon the local church.

I cannot help thinking that here we find one of the most important elements of his success. By leaving the church to decide who should be admitted, he established firmly the great principle of mutual responsibility. The church was a brotherhood, and the brethren suffered if any improper person was admitted to their society. They knew the candidates intimately. They were in the best possible position to judge who were fit and proper candidates. That they might make mistakes, and that they did make great mistakes, is sufficiently obvious; but if they made mistakes, they made them at their own peril. In this matter of mutual responsibility a little practical experience is worth a great weight of verbal teaching.

In our modern missionary practice we have constantly, almost invariably, violated this principle. We have constantly thrown the whole responsibility for the administration of baptism upon a foreign teacher who, as a stranger, is in the worst possible position to judge the real motives and character of those who offer themselves for baptism, and by so doing we have done much to weaken the sense of mutual responsibility among our converts. We have taught them that the church is a brotherhood, and that they must all work together for the good of the whole, but in practice we have denied their right and their duty to exercise that responsibility, and that at a most vital point.

It is true that we commonly require native sponsors. But it can hardly, I think, be said that we have by that requirement succeeded in throwing the real responsibility of admission upon the local church. If a man has been prepared, or examined, and accepted by the priest in charge, the mere fact that he has been so accepted exercises an overwhelming influence over the minds of an oriental congregation. They will not appear to resist the authority of their spiritual masters; and where, as is sometimes the case, the priest claims, or readily accepts, sole responsibility for the administration of the sacrament, they naturally allow the claim. It is a very extreme action to oppose the baptism of a man, whom the priest in charge has declared his willingness to accept.

Many a man has been baptized who would not have been admitted if the whole body of the church had realized that the responsibility for his admission rested with them, and had had opportunity to express their opinion in their own way. Even as it is, men sometimes fail to find sponsors, though we can at the moment perceive no reason why they should fail; but such cases are, I fancy, rare. I cannot see what we gain by assuming the responsibility, and acting on our own authority in these matters. We are often left to act in much doubt and perplexity. The unworthy are not always rejected or sent back for further teaching; the worthy are not always accepted. We do not avoid the dangers of mistaken judgments, we rob the people of the right and duty of expressing themselves and so exercising and realizing by exercise their mutual responsibility one for another. I should like to see it accepted as a general principle that converts should be presented by members of the church to the church, and accepted by the church and baptized on the authority of the whole local church acting as a church.

As with the admission of converts, so with the appointment of elders, there was some responsibility recognized by the brethren. I cannot here enter upon the question of the meaning and form of ordination in the early Church; I am dealing only with the method which St Paul practised in the appointment of elders in the churches of his foundation. There is no doubt that he did appoint elders;[1] and it seems to be equally clear that he did not appoint simply on his own initiative, acting on his own private judgment. This is borne out by the constant emphasis laid upon 'good report', and by the term which St Luke employs to describe his action. As in the case of 'the seven' at Jerusalem, so in the Four Provinces there was some form of election.

But it may be argued that the evidence for election is not sufficient, and that St Paul did in the first instance appoint elders simply on his

[1] Acts 14. 23.

own authority and judgment. In that case the parallel to his administration of baptism will be even more exact. For, as we shall see later,
the elders appointed by St Paul had authority to ordain as well as to
baptize. If then the first elders were appointed simply by St Paul
they must be compared with the first converts who were baptized by
St Paul. Just as he baptized three or four and then committed the
responsibility for admitting others to those whom he had baptized;
so he ordained three or four and committed the authority for ordaining others into their hands.

There is not a shred of evidence that any congregation created its
own elders by election alone. There is evidence that congregations
did have some say in the election of elders. There is evidence that St
Paul did commit authority to appoint elders to others (notably to
Timothy and Titus), and that this authority very early became
concentrated in the hands of a single local bishop. But the right of
the congregation to have some say in the appointment is manifest
throughout the period with which we are dealing. By this means the
principle of mutual responsibility was again made prominent.

Futhermore, this principle was maintained by the fact that St
Paul ordained as elders members of the church to which they
belonged. He did not establish a provincial school to which all
candidates for ordination must go, and from which they might be
sent to minister to congregations in any part of the province, at the
bidding of a central committee or at his own. The elders were really
of the church to which they ministered. They were at home. They
were known to the members of their flock. If they received any
pecuniary support, they received it from men who supported them
because they felt the need of their undivided and uninterrupted
care. Thus the bond between the elders and the church to which
they ministered was extremely close.

This is of the utmost importance. It makes a great difference if the
ministers feel some responsibility to those to whom they minister,
and if the general congregation feels some responsibility for the
character and work of those who are set over them. Where candidates
for the ministry are selected by the superior order, where they are
ordained solely on the authority of the superior order, and are
appointed to their posts by the sole direction of the superior order,
those who are so appointed are apt to lose any sense of responsibility
to the congregation among whom they minister, and the congre-

gation feels no responsibility for them. The result is an inevitable weakening of what should be the strongest support, both to clergy and laity. Where the superior order consists almost wholly of foreigners, the result is often deplorable. The catechists, teachers, deacons, and priests, so sent out, are wholly independent of the one authority which they really understand, native public opinion; solely dependent upon the one authority which they seldom can understand, the foreign missionary. Consequently they are always striving to act as they think will please the foreigners, they imitate them as closely as possible, they fear to take any independent action, whilst the members of the congregation on their side feel that they have nothing to do with their appointment. They accept their ministrations so long as they are not seriously offended; they tolerate, but they do not support them; and if anything goes wrong, they disclaim all responsibility.

The elders so appointed were not young. They were apparently selected because they were men of high moral character, sober, grave, men of weight and reputation. When St Paul ordained younger men, as Timothy, he took them away with him to act as his assistants and ministers that they might receive from him deeper lessons of Christian doctrine and practice than they could learn at home; but, in the provinces, he ordained, to be the first leaders of the Church, men who thoroughly understood the condition and requirements of their congregations, men who were respected by the congregations for their moral and social position.

They were not necessarily highly educated men, they cannot have had any profound knowledge of Christian doctrine. It is impossible that St Paul can have required from them any knowledge of Hebrew, or of any foreign language. From the evidence set forth above, it seems unlikely that he could have required any great acquaintance with the life and teachings of Christ. It is not probable that he expected or demanded any profound knowledge of Greek philosophy. It is inevitable that he must have been satisfied with a somewhat limited general education, and with a more or less meagre acquaintance with the Septuagint and with his mystical interpretation of it, with a knowledge of the brief outline of Christian doctrine set forth in the Epistle to the Thessalonians, and some instruction in the meaning and method of administration of the two sacraments of baptism and the Lord's Supper.

The qualifications of elders were primarily moral.[1] If they added to moral qualifications intellectual qualifications so much the better, but high intellectual qualifications were not deemed necessary. Very early there grew up a class of teachers who by virtue of their spiritual insight into the meaning of the Old Testament, or the sayings of Christ known to them, occupied a place of great importance in the Church; but they were not necessarily elders. This is the state of affairs depicted in the Didaché,[2] and the Didascalia agrees with this. 'If it be possible let him (the bishop) be a teacher, or if he be illiterate, let him be persuasive and wise of speech: let him be advanced in years.'[3]

They were not an inferior order. 'Upon the whole,' says Professor

[1] It has been urged upon me that in dealing with the qualifications of elders I have omitted one, and that the most important, namely, that they should be men of 'cleansed heart, a good conscience and *unfeigned* FAITH'. I have omitted this deliberately, because St Paul omitted it. In the great passages (1 Tim. 3. 2–10 and Tit. 1. 6–9), in which he sets forth the qualifications necessary for bishops and deacons there is not one word about 'a cleansed heart', or even of 'a good conscience' or of 'unfeigned faith' in the sense in which I understand my critic to use these words. All that St Paul demands is morality of conduct and honest acceptance of the Creed. The truth is that if we try to judge the spiritual condition of men's souls before God, or to estimate their spiritual fitness for work here by any other test than morality of life and readiness to confess the doctrine, we fail. Every society which has tried to set up any other test has failed. They have all admitted men who have failed both in morals and in doctrine.

Nevertheless, there is a real truth underlying the criticism. Neither moral qualities nor readiness to profess belief in the doctrine, in themselves, necessarily imply faith in Jesus Christ, nor do they always prove that their possessor is conscious of the grace of the Holy Spirit, and this consciousness is a matter of real importance for a minister in the Church of God. The man who celebrates the mysteries should be conscious of the grace. There is a real meaning in the demand for spiritual men for spiritual work. It is a fact that some men reveal, in speech and act, a sense of the reality of spiritual things which others do not possess, and that these are the men who are best qualified to help others. This cannot be reduced to rule, but it can and it ought to influence us in our administration of the rite of ordination more than it does. We often refuse to ordain men, who certainly and plainly possess this qualification, because they do not possess the far less important qualification of intellectual ability; whilst we accept men who possess the inferior qualifications in spite of the fact that they manifestly lack this all-important one. St Paul did not tell Timothy and Titus to ignore spiritual qualifications. He simply refused to set up a test of the candidates' spiritual state before God, which he knew men could not properly apply, whilst he insisted upon a test of his state before the Church which men could easily apply. The inward state must be judged only by the outward act, whether the man was moral, and held the faithful word which was according to the teaching. The test was a test of life and speech.

[2] See *Didaché*, ch. xv.

[3] *Didascalia Ap.*, trans. Mrs Gibson, p. 23.

Gwatkin, 'their position and duties (apart from the question of a possible superior) are not unlike those of the priest as described in the English Ordinal.'[1] Their duty was to look after and care for the general well-being of the body, and to administer the Sacraments. The Sacraments unquestionably were administered in the churches founded by St Paul; and I take it for granted that they could not be administered indiscriminately by any convert. In saying this I do not wish it to be supposed that I deny that prophets and inspired men celebrated the mysteries and exercised very wide powers. I am simply asserting that the elders appointed, either by St Paul or under his direction, did exercise these powers. The importance of the ordination of elders lay in this, that when a church was equipped with elders, it possessed not merely leaders, but men properly appointed to see that the Sacraments, without which it would have been starved in its spiritual life and crippled in the work of expansion, were duly performed.

They were indeed of an order different from that which we now call priesthood, and in one respect higher. They not only administered Sacraments: they ordained others; for there is no suggestion that St Paul ever ordained a second time in any church of his foundation. Moreover, we read that the churches grew in Paul's absence, and we know by name at least one organized church of which St Paul himself says that he had not seen the members.[2] There is no reason to suppose that these new churches were destitute of ministers and sacraments, nor is there any account of special ordinations of special ministers for them. Either, then, they received the sacraments at the hands of spiritual persons who were recognized as spiritual pastors in virtue of their charismatic gifts, or their ministers were appointed by those whom St Paul had ordained in the churches directly established by him. Without excluding the possibility of the former alternative in some cases, I think that the evidence inclines us to accept the latter as the general rule. Later in his career St Paul specially appointed Timothy and others to exercise what we should today call episcopal functions; but in the ten years now under consideration we hear of no such apostolic bishops. Nevertheless the practice of St Paul himself, and the inference to be drawn from all the known cases of ordination, lead us to believe that it was an accepted

[1] *Early Church History*, vol. 1, p. 69.
[2] Col. 2. 1.

principle that authority to administer Sacraments was not left to the individual claim of any person who might assume it, nor given by mere election, but was definitely conferred by those who could show that they themselves had been appointed by the Lord to perform such acts. Consequently, it seems to be an irresistible conclusion that the elders appointed by St Paul were definitely appointed with power to add to their number and thus to secure to new churches a proper order and certainty of sacramental grace.

Finally, St Paul was not content with ordaining one elder for each church. In every place he ordained several. This ensured that all authority should not be concentrated in the hands of one man. It ensured the possibility of frequent administrations of the Sacraments. The infant church was not left to depend for its spiritual sustenance upon the weakness of a single individual. Responsibility was divided and many were enlisted in the service of the church. Thus the whole body grew together. As the general knowledge increased, the older men died, and younger men, who had grown up with the new generation and shared their education and experience, gradually took their place and became the natural leaders and the ordained successors of their fathers, whilst young teachers who had a gift for preaching found their opportunities and their experience in the open services of the church.

In our day, on the contrary, there has been a tendency to concentrate all functions in the fewest possible hands. The same man is priest and teacher and administrator, sometimes architect and builder as well. We have set up a purely artificial standard of learning as the necessary qualification for the ministry. We have required a long and expensive college education as a preparation even for the office of deacon. We have taken the youngest men and trained them to occupy the position of authority, such very limited authority as a native may exercise under the supervision of a foreign priest-in-charge.

The examination test is made the real test of fitness for the priesthood. Moral qualifications may suffice for the office of catechist, but if a man is to proceed further he must pass an examination of a very artificial character. In other words we select by examination. That system has long been tried, and is already being seriously questioned at home, and it does not seem to appeal to oriental minds as reasonable. In an address presented to the Lieutenant-Governor by the leaders of the Muslim community of the Punjab in 1904, they said:

> We presume that you English had your reasons for imposing such tests: we do not know and cannot guess them. The system is repugnant to old traditions, and we cannot consider the results of examinations as furnishing sufficient evidence of a man's aptitude to govern or to dispense justice. Our history has shown us that there are other criteria. To cursory examinations, in which memory plays a predominant part, we prefer the presumptions which arise on the social position of the candidate, the services rendered to the State by his family, his own character and demeanour, and his aptitude to obey and command.[1]

Of course in our selection of candidates for Orders, we do not rely wholly upon examinations. The candidate must bear a good moral character. But the fact remains that we have made too much of the intellectual test. That objection has been repeated by many missionaries—not only evangelistic, but educational. When we are constantly engaged in criticising the method of our Civil Governors in such a matter as this, it seems absurd that we should continue to imitate what we so often condemn.

Four very serious consequences have followed upon our action:

(1) The people have been deprived of the Sacraments. Our mission priests have often large numbers of communicants scattered over a very wide area, entirely dependent upon them for the administration of the Sacraments, with the result that the people have opportunity to receive the Sacraments only at rare intervals. These priests have often under them many excellent and devoted catechists[2] who cannot be ordained, solely because they have not had a college education. Thus we deny the Bread of Life to people whom we teach to believe that partaking of the Bread of Life is the first duty of the Christian, and the first necessity for spiritual growth. It requires no great education to be able to celebrate the Holy Mysteries. We

[1] Quoted by Chailley, *Admin. Problems in British India*, p. 550.
[2] An excellent example of this is to be found in the *Church Abroad* for May 1910. There the Rev. E. Hill tells the story of a most devoted African Christian named Josiah Ngcombo and ends his story: 'As one stands before his grave one feels how cheap and vulgar is this shallow-pated criticism which says you can't make a native a genuine Christian or fit to be a minister.' Yet Josiah Ngcombo was a catechist working under a priest whom he called his 'Boss'. Such instances might be multiplied indefinitely. One feels tempted to correct Mr Hill's conclusion and to say, 'As one reads his story one feels how cheap and vulgar is this shallow-pated criticism which says that you can't make a native a priest unless he has been to college.'

have put intellectual qualifications in the first place, with the result that the congregations starve whilst we educate a few young men.

(2) The young men so educated are sometimes, by that very education, out of touch with their congregations. They return to their people with strange ideas and strange habits. They are lonely, and they have to struggle against the perils of loneliness. They are not even the best teachers of people from whose intellectual and spiritual life they have so long been absent. They do not know how to answer their difficulties or to supply their necessities. They know so much Christian doctrine and philosophy that they have forgotten the religion of their country.[1] The congregation has not grown with them, nor they with the congregation. They come, as it were, from outside, and only a few exceptional men can learn to overcome that difficulty.

(3) The grave men of the church, the natural leaders of the village life, and the natural leaders of the church are silenced. The church is not led and administered by the people to whom all would naturally turn, but either by a foreigner, or by a young man who has come with a foreign education. In this way a great source of strength is lost. The real elders of the community are not elders in the church, and the whole church suffers in consequence.

(4) The natural teacher, the divinely gifted preacher, is silenced. The only teacher is the foreign-educated minister. There is no opportunity for the church to find its prophets, nor for the prophets to find themselves. The prophet is in danger either of losing his gift or of leaving the church in order to find opportunity for its exercise.

This is not to say that there is no place for the foreign-educated teacher. He may be said to resemble in some respects the young ministers whom St Paul educated in his own society by constant association with himself. Carefully selected and diligently trained, these men might go about as preachers and teachers of deeper truths and higher knowledge, the messengers of, and fellow-workers with, the white missionary, who, relieved of the overwhelming burden of personal ministration to numbers of small congregations over a vast area, could constantly be in touch with his churches, and yet have opportunity to open up new centres of work. It is absolutely essential that the founder of churches should keep in close touch with the communities which he has established, so that he may be able at

---

[1] In some of our colleges we even find it necessary to teach the elements of the native religion in order that our pastors may not be absolutely ignorant of it.

any moment to intervene in any crisis or serious difficulty which may arise. St Paul needed Timothy and Titus, and we sorely need zealous and capable lieutenants whom we can despatch with haste to any point of our missions where the less educated and less trained leaders may be in danger of falling into error. We need such fellow-workers not only to help us in directing the infant communities; we need them also to help us in breaking new ground. It is in working with them in evangelistic tours that we can best train them both before and after they leave college, and in evangelistic tours they may be of great service in instructing inquirers.

Four things, then, we see St Paul deemed necessary for the establishment of his churches, and only four. A tradition or elementary Creed, the Sacraments of Baptism and the Holy Communion, Orders, and the Holy Scriptures. He trained his converts in the simplest and most practical form. He delivered these to them. He exercised them as a body in the understanding and practice of them, and he left them to work them out for themselves as a body whilst he himself went on with his own special work. He was ready at any moment to encourage or direct them by messengers, by letters, or by personal visits, as they needed direction or encouragement; but he neither desired, nor attempted, to stay with them, or to establish his ministers amongst them to do for them what he was determined that they must learn to do for themselves. He knew the essential elements, and he trained his converts in those and in those alone, and he trained them by teaching them to use what he gave them.

PART IV

St Paul's Method of Dealing with Organized Churches

Authority and Discipline

AUTHORITY

With the appointment of elders the churches were complete. They were fully equipped. They very soon became familiar with all the orders of ministry both permanent and charismatic.[1] They no longer depended necessarily upon St Paul. If he went away, or if he died, the churches remained. They grew in numbers and in grace: they were centres of spiritual light by which the darkness of surrounding heathenism was gradually dispelled. In Galatia 'the churches were strengthened in the faith and increased in number daily'.[2] From Thessalonica 'the word of the Lord sounded out'[3] in Macedonia and Achaia. From Ephesus the Gospel spread throughout all the neighbouring country so that many churches sprang up, the members of which had never seen St Paul's face, and he himself could write to the Romans that he had 'no more place in those regions'.[4]

They were no longer dependent upon the Apostle, but they were not independent of him. When there was occasion he did not hesitate to assert authority over the churches which he had founded and to claim that he had received it directly from the Lord. 'Though I should glory somewhat abundantly concerning our authority, which the Lord gave for building you up and not for casting you down, I shall not be put to shame.'[5] When he thought it necessary he could stop the mouth of an objector with the assertion, 'We have no such custom'.[6] He laid down the general principle, 'As the Lord hath distributed to every man, as God hath called each, so let him walk', and added, 'So ordain I in all the churches'.[7] He gave certain directions for public worship, and concluded, 'The rest will I set in order

[1] 1 Cor. 12. 28.
[2] Acts 16. 5.
[3] 1 Thess. 1. 8.
[4] Rom. 15. 23.
[5] 2 Cor. 10. 8, cf. 13. 10.
[6] 1 Cor. 11. 16.
[7] 1 Cor. 7. 17.

when I come'.[1] When people resisted his authority, he proposed to set up a court in which every word should be established 'at the mouth of two or three witnesses', with the threat 'If I come again I will not spare'.[2]

Now with regard to these assertions of the apostolic authority, it is necessary to observe that they all occur in the epistles to one church, and that they were called forth for the most part by the outrageous conduct of unreasonable and disorderly men. They certainly do not represent St Paul's general attitude to his churches. They do not even represent the attitude of St Paul to the Corinthians as a body. In the very epistles in which these threats are used, he repudiates the idea that he had 'lordship over their faith'.[3] Though they certainly prove that the Apostle recognized that he possessed a power upon which he could fall back in case of necessity, yet they also prove how sparingly he used it. He had to deal with some of the most pressing and difficult problems which can agitate a church, many of them problems most easily and effectively solved, as we should naturally suppose, by an appeal to authority, yet he scarcely ever lays down the law, preferring doubt and strife to an enforced obedience to a rule. It is important that we should examine these cases carefully, because they give us a most valuable insight into the method of the Apostle and greatly help us to understand the secret of his success.

The most important questions which came before him were those of personal purity, litigation, and the eating of things offered to idols.

(1) *Fornication.* The prevalence of sexual immorality in the Gentile world was one of the difficulties which most grievously vexed the Jewish party in the Church. They argued with perfect reason that if Gentiles were admitted into the Church without being compelled to keep the law of Moses, the moral condition of the Church would soon be dragged down to a very low standard: and when they failed to enforce the duty of observing the whole Mosaic Code upon the Gentile Christians, they succeeded in making this offence the subject of one of the four solemn decrees of the Jerusalem Council.

The event proved how just their anxiety was. St Paul had scarcely

[1] 1 Cor. 11. 34.
[2] 2 Cor. 13. 1-2.
[3] 2 Cor. 1. 24.

ceased preaching at Thessalonica, he had been in constant communication with the church when he wrote his first epistle: yet the sins of fornication and adultery occupy the first place in his exhortations.[1] He had not been absent from Corinth more than two and a half years when he wrote the first Epistle to the Corinthians; yet in spite of the fact that the church had enjoyed the instruction of Apollos and was notorious for the wealth of its spiritual gifts, it is perfectly manifest that fornication was a common offence.

How then did St Paul deal with this very serious difficulty? There is not in his letters one word of law: there is not a hint that the Jerusalem Council had issued any decree on the subject: there is not a suggestion that he desires a code of rules or a table of penalties. He does not threaten offenders with punishment. He does not say that he shall take any steps to procure their correction. He beseeches and exhorts in the Lord people to whom the Holy Spirit has been given to surrender themselves to the guidance of that Holy Spirit, to recognize that He is given to them that they may be holy in body and in soul, and that uncleanness necessarily involves the rejection of the Holy Spirit and incurs the wrath of God.

In the Epistle to the Thessalonians,[2] for instance, this is his argument. He reminds his readers of his personal teaching when he was amongst them. He reminds them that God's will for them is sanctification. He suggests that there should be a difference between the conduct of Christians and that of Gentiles who know not God. He warns them that the Lord is the avenger of such misdeeds. He reiterates the truth that the purpose and will of God in calling them from the heathen world was that they should be made holy. Finally he warns them that the rejection of his teaching on this subject is the rejection of the Holy Spirit.

Precisely similar is the language which he uses in the Epistle to the Corinthians. It has indeed been argued that he does in one verse apparently recommend that fornicators should be excommunicated when he says, 'I write unto you not to keep company, if any man that is named a brother be a fornicator'.[3] But this certainly does not

---

[1] 1 Thess. 4. 1–8. The exhortations do not begin till chap. 4 and begin with 'Finally', as if they were last in the Apostle's thought. But that does not alter the fact that in the exhortations the warnings against adultery and fornication take the most important place.

[2] 1 Thess. 4. 1–8.

[3] 1 Cor. 5. 11.

refer to formal excommunication, because it includes not only fornicators, but covetous, and revilers and extortioners, as well as drunkards and idolaters; and the same word is used of association both with heathen and with Christians.[1] It is an exhortation to good Christians to use their private influence to correct the faults of their brethren by the silent rebuke of avoiding their company. It is to be compared rather with the exhortation in the second Epistle to the Thessalonians, 'We command you, brethren, in the name of the Lord Jesus Christ that ye withdraw yourselves from every brother that walketh disorderly and not after the tradition which they received of us',[2] than with the direction to 'Purge out the old leaven' and to 'deliver the offender to Satan'. The one is an exhortation 'to send a man to Coventry'; the other 'to expel him'.

Setting aside then this point, the language which St Paul uses elsewhere in the Epistle to the Corinthians is exactly the same in character as that which we found in the Epistle to the Thessalonians. He argues that fornication is a violation of the true use of the body,[3] that it is contrary to the glorious hope of the Resurrection, that it is a desecration of the members of Christ, that the body is not the Christian's own to use as he pleases, but is a temple of the Holy Ghost.

Surely it is very strange that St Paul should not even hint at the fact that this sin had been condemned by the Jerusalem Council. Surely it is strange that in speaking of fornication in close connection with a flagrant case of incest he should not even suggest that it is a breach of the Ten Commandments. It is plain that St Paul did not appeal to law at all. He did not seek the source of the moral life in any command or any exercise of authority. His Gospel was not a gospel of law but of spirit.

In this he was following the example of Christ Himself. It has often been pointed out that the method of Jesus was to inculcate principles and to leave His disciples to apply them; and it is interesting to observe that as St Paul followed Christ so Clement of Rome kept the same rule in his Epistle to the Corinthians. It is a striking characteristic of that epistle that the writer never forgets that his duty is to point out the right course of action rather than to lay

[1] 1 Cor. 5. 9. cf. ver. 11.
[2] 2 Thess. 3. 6.
[3] 1 Cor. 6. 13–19.

commands upon the church to which he writes. Again and again he expresses his firm conviction that the church knows the will of God and will surrender itself to the guidance of the Spirit.[1]

But it may be said that the church in Corinth was of such an independent spirit and was so conscious of its own capacities that it would not have tolerated any more autocratic method of government. The Corinthians were in no temper to accept directions simply on the authority even of St Paul. That is, of course, true. But the question is, how did they come to that mind? If at conversion they had been admitted to a church and initiated into a religion, of which the most marked requirement was observance of law as laid down by authority, they would have understood that they could not be Christians unless they submitted to authority. Submission and obedience would have been the chief duty inculcated. Observance of the rules would have been the first duty of every convert. If St Paul had from the very beginning insisted upon this aspect of the church that it is a society governed by rules which every one who enters it must keep, the Corinthians and all his converts would never have thought of it in any other way. But that would have been precisely what St Paul did not believe, and therefore could not teach. If he had begun in that way the difficulties which arose in Corinth could not have taken the form which they did take, and St Paul could not possibly have dealt with them in the way in which he did deal with them. There might have been an insurrection against authority, but it would have been a revolt against the whole church system, and St Paul must have suppressed it by authority, or the Church would have lost Corinth.

(2) *Litigation.* Some of the Corinthian Christians had apparently been prosecuting their brethren in the heathen law courts. Obviously this was an offence likely to bring the Name into disrepute. The simplest way to deal with it would have been to forbid it by decree, and to threaten any offender in future with penalties. But that is not how St Paul deals with it. He reasons with the whole body, and sets before the brethren his argument, and there leaves the matter. He puts before them the glaring inconsistency between their conduct and their position as Christians. It is, he says, unworthy of men, who are called to be judges of the world and of angels, to drag their brethren before a heathen judge. It speaks ill, he says, of the wisdom and moral

---

[1] *Ep. of Clement to Cor.*, especially chap. 40. 1; 45, 2 f.; 53, 1; 63, 3.

tone of the church if there cannot be found in it one who can decide questions in dispute. He urges upon them that it would be better to suffer injury than thus to publish the immorality of the church, whilst to injure and defraud the brethren is to make themselves as the heathen. He warns them that such shall not inherit the Kingdom of God.[1]

What could be less like legislation for the church? It is not the part of a legislator to argue, or to exhort the injured party to suffer in silence rather than bring discredit upon the body. St Paul does not legislate, neither does he urge them to legislate, he appeals to the Spirit in them. He does not suggest that he will take any action if they refuse, as some of them certainly would refuse, to listen to his arguments. For them he has no threat of action to be taken on his part, only a warning that sinners will be excluded from the Kingdom.

(3) *Eating of things offered to idols*.[2] At the Jerusalem Council it had been decreed that the Gentile Christians should abstain from things sacrificed to idols. At Corinth some of them not only ate things sacrificed to idols: they attended feasts in the idol's temple,[3] a far more flagrant offence, and one which brought many other offences in its train. A feast in a temple was associated not only with idolatry, but too often with impurity also. Surely on such a subject it would be right to appeal to the decree of the Council, and to close all mouths with the word 'Forbidden'.

St Paul on the contrary not only does not legislate himself, he makes no reference to any law on the subject. No one who was not acquainted with the decree of the Jerusalem Council from some other source would guess from St Paul's treatment of the subject that such a decree existed. He not only does not quote it, he does not even maintain it.[4] In Corinth it was a disputed point whether it was

---

[1] 1 Cor. 6. 1–11.

[2] 1 Cor. 8.

[3] 1 Cor. 8. 10.

[4] It has been argued (a) from the silence of St Paul with respect to the decree, (b) from the inconsistency of his language with the terms of it, that the account given in the Acts is unhistorical. It is not necessary for me to enter upon this discussion. Where Harnack, and Sanday, and Ramsay agree on the generally historical nature of a document, I may accept it without excuse. But if my contention is admitted, it destroys the ground of the objection made against the account given in the Acts. It is admitted that the ground of attack is the difficulty of reconciling the language of St Paul with the language of the decree. I venture to suggest that this demand for agreement is a striking illustration of the legal character of

lawful to eat of the sacrifices. St Paul does not decide the question. It is quite plain that he does not approve of the practice. 'I would not that ye should have communion with devils.'[1] But he speaks, 'as to wise men, judge ye what I say'. He appeals to the spirit of charity. Some, he says, have knowledge and know that the idol is nothing and can eat things sacrificed to idols without acknowledging the idol as a god. They are not conscious of the idol, they feel themselves superior to such vanities. But others still retain something of their former superstition. They cannot escape from the sense that the idol really is something to be feared. They cannot escape from the sense that when they share in an idolatrous feast they do actually bring themselves into communion with the idol deity. Their conscience revolts and is distressed, but they are ashamed to refuse to do what other bolder and more enlightened brethren do. They eat, and suffer the pangs of an evil conscience. They feel that they have sinned against Christ by sharing in the service of an idol.[2]

St Paul then appeals to the highest Christian virtue in his readers. He contrasts knowledge and charity. He says that to rely upon knowledge, to seize the liberty of pure enlightenment of the mind, to demonstrate the truth at all hazards and in every way and by any means, is not Christian. He subordinates knowledge to charity. He argues that charity must come first, and that if acts based upon knowledge injure and mislead the weak, they are not only not praiseworthy, they are sinful. To injure the consciences of the weaker brethren is to sin against Christ.

We cannot even imagine a modern European missionary acting like that. If any of his converts showed a tendency to kow-tow to the tablet of Confucius on the ground that they knew quite well that Confucius was only a man, and that the act was only one of respectful

---

our modern ideas of the Church, and that the inconsistency is only a singular example of the method of St Paul. As for the dispute concerning the original form of the decree, that has no importance for my argument. If it is admitted that there was *any* decree, the terms of it unquestionably included fornication and idolatry, and if those two are acknowledged, my argument stands. For if in the decree, 'Participation in the idolatrous feasts is especially emphasized, simply because this was the crassest form of idolatry' (Harnack, *Acts of the Apostles*, trans. J. R. Wilkinson, Crown Theol. Library, p. 257); then the argument of St Paul in this place, if not actually at variance with it, still ignores it in the most marked and singular manner.

[1] 1 Cor. 10. 14–22.
[2] 1 Cor. 8, 4–7.

I   117

recognition of his virtue as a teacher of the nation, would he write a letter leaving them to judge on principles of charity whether they should continue to do so or not? Or would he rather hasten to judge the question in consultation with his fellow European missionaries, perhaps not even consulting any native Christians at all, and issue a rule for the church? If he were a Roman Catholic would he not appeal to the decree of Pope Clement XI and say the question had been settled?

In our dealings with our native converts we habitually appeal to law. We attempt to administer a code which is alien to the thought of the people with whom we have to deal, we appeal to precedents which are no precedents to them, and we quote decisions of which our hearers do not understand either the history or the reason. Without satisfying their minds or winning the consent of their consciences, we settle all questions with a word.

This is unfortunate because it leaves the people unconvinced and uneducated, and teaches them the habit of unreasoning obedience. They learn to expect law and to delight in the exact fulfilment of precise and minute directions. By this method we make it difficult to stir the consciences of our converts, when it is most important that their consciences should be stirred. Bereft of exact directions, they are helpless. They cease to expect to understand the reason of things, or to exercise their intelligence. Instead of seeking the illumination of the Holy Ghost they prefer to trust to formal instructions from their foreign guides. The consequence is that when their foreign guide cannot, or will not, supply precise commands, they pay little attention to his godly exhortations. Counsels which have no precedent behind them seem weak. Anything which is not in open disobedience to a law can be tolerated. Appeals to principles appear vague and difficult. They are not accustomed to the labour of thinking them out and applying them. If a missionary explains to his converts that some act is not in harmony with the mind of Christ his words fall on deaf ears: if he tells them that it was forbidden in a council of such and such a date, they obey him; but that is the way of death not of life; it is Judaism not Christianity; it is papal not Pauline.

St Paul cannot have believed that by his appeal to charity the question would be settled. He must have foreseen strife and division. He must have deliberately preferred strife and division, heart-burnings, and distresses, and failures, to laying down a law. He saw that it was better that his converts should win their way to security by many falls than that he should try to make a short cut for them. He valued a single act of willing self-surrender, for the sake of the Gospel, above the external peace of a sullen or unintelligent acceptance of a rule.

By this refusal to prejudge the question of the presence of Christians in idol temples, St Paul avoided one great difficulty which constantly besets us in our work. He made it possible for converts to continue to work at their trades as members of a heathen guild or society. It is perfectly clear that the Christians in the Four Provinces of whom very many, if not the majority, were of the commercial or artisan classes, did not abandon their labour in workshops where heathen rites were performed. Such of them as were slaves could not escape from their attendance at heathen functions, and probably most of those who were free men could have done so only at great loss. They were present, but they did not partake. Tertullian in his treatise *de Idolatria*, shows that there was scarcely a trade or business in which a Christian could engage without being mixed up with idolatry in some form or other, but there was not in the Four Provinces any immediate break. Christians did not feel it their duty to live in idleness and beggary rather than work at their old trades. St Paul did not feel it necessary to forbid them from continuing at their trades from fear lest they should be drawn back into the gulf of heathenism from which they were hardly escaped. New-born Christians and their children were not withdrawn from their heathen surroundings into the seclusion of a select society which had nothing to do with the outside world. They did not establish Christian villages from which idolatry might be excluded. They did not withdraw their children from heathen schools from fear lest they might be led astray into idolatry. There must indeed have been some who in those early days sacrificed their living rather than continue in trades which were directly and definitely associated with the practice of idolatry, and very soon the Church began to make some provision for such persons left penniless by their adherence to the doctrine of Christ. But for the most part it was not necessary for Christians to forsake their work because idolatrous rites were practised in their workshops.

With us there is a tendency manifest to encourage that kind of separation, a physical separation from a heathen society. Our converts often cease to live in a heathen society. Sometimes this is involuntary, because they are expelled by the heathen; but sometimes it is voluntary. They congregate in Christian villages, they are put into Christian workshops, they cease to work under heathen masters. Christian schools are provided for their children, which heathen scholars may indeed attend, but where the teaching is strictly Christian.

By this we have gained something and we have lost something. We have gained an immunity from temptation. Our converts enjoy the privileges and support of Christian intercourse; it is more easy to watch over them; the children grow up as Christians without being called upon to face the fiery ordeal of the heathen school and workshop. But on the other hand we have lost something: the Christians cannot so leaven society when they are, as it were, outside it, as they can when they are really in it, living the same life, sharing the same toil, the same gains, the same losses, as their heathen fellows; they and their religion are peculiarly the care of the foreign missionary; they are looked upon as having separated themselves from the life of the nation; their religion does not appear to belong to their people.

Of course I know that this criticism has always in every age been directed against Christians. They cannot escape from it, however much they live in their nation. They must always be a peculiar and suspect people. But if they are separated and collected in little groups of their own, that criticism has a keener edge and bites more sharply, and they do not, and cannot, so readily influence their fellows. Besides this the converts themselves, separated from their fellows, tend to lean more heavily upon the foreign missionary. They learn to imitate him more closely, to expect more and more support from him, to adopt more and more Western habits. They get out of touch with their heathen neighbours. The missionary, too, suffers somewhat. By ministering constantly to Christian communities, he, too, fails to attain or to maintain a close intercourse with the heathen round him. It is more easy to deal with his converts in groups and to keep a close hold upon them; but it is less easy to avoid the danger of over-much direction. It becomes more easy to minister, more difficult to evangelize. I do not wish to lay too much stress upon this or to exaggerate it; but, seeing that the besetting sin of European missionaries is the love of administration, I wish to suggest that this tendency to separate converts into groups apart from the native life around them is not without its dangers and disadvantages, and to point out that St Paul rather laid stress upon a spiritual separation than upon a physical separation from an idolatrous society.

(4) *Marriage and Divorce.* But it may perhaps be said that there is one subject of the first importance upon which St Paul does very distinctly lay down the law. It may be argued that the whole of the seventh chapter of the first Epistle to the Corinthians dealing with marriage is written in a tone of authority. In answer to this it must be observed, first, that the chapter is expressly written in answer to an appeal for guidance, secondly, that St Paul is here extremely careful to distinguish between the command of the Lord and his own judgment, and, thirdly, that the treatment of the marriage question is very incomplete, and on some points singularly inconclusive.

For instance, he seems to lay it down as a principle that if widows marry again, it must be 'in the Lord',[1] that is, presumably, with Christians, but he does not insist on this in dealing with the marriage of virgins. Finally, where he most distinctly lays down a law and claims for it the authority of Christ,[2] he yet issues directions for the conduct of the person who acts contrary to the law which he has just asserted.[3] Thus it would appear that throughout the chapter he is rather expressing his own view of what is desirable than legislating for the Church, and though he expresses himself in definite clear-cut directions, yet for the most part he does so with reasons given which he evidently intends to be weighed as arguments tending to support his expression of opinion.

I cannot help concluding, from these characteristic notes, that this chapter is not really an exception to the general rule which we have hitherto found to dominate the Apostle's attitude to the church. He avoids in every possible way making clear-cut legal demands which must be obeyed in the letter. He rather suggests principles and trusts to the Spirit which dwells in the church to apply them.

DISCIPLINE

Nevertheless, when individuals broke through all bounds and

[1] 1 Cor. 7. 39.
[2] Ver. 10.
[3] Ver. 11. See Robertson and Plummer in *International Critical Commentary*, ad loc.

committed flagrant offences he did not hesitate to insist upon the need of discipline. There is a point at which the conscience of the whole Church ought to be stirred to protest, when for the Church to pass over an offence in silence is to deny her claim to be a moral society. It is in just such cases that the Church is often slow to act. Comparatively small offences are sometimes visited with stern severity: horrible crimes shock the whole congregation, but none dares to move.

Such an offence was committed at Corinth, and Christians who wrote letters to St Paul to inquire what they should do in the case of members of the church who wished to live a life of continence against the will of their partners,[1] took no action themselves and apparently did not mention the subject to the Apostle. St Paul could not avoid moving in the matter, but he obviously did so with great reluctance. It is quite clear that he was determined in the last resort to take action himself, but it is equally clear that he was most anxious to avoid it. He wished the church to realize its responsibility, and to act as a body. In his epistle he did not tell the church what penalty it ought to enforce, he did not write to exhort the offender to submit. He wrote to accuse the church of its failure to realize its duty in the matter. In a case of this kind, according to his view, the church, as a church, had a duty to perform, a duty to the offender and a duty to itself. To shirk that duty was criminal. Therefore he waited to see if the church would do its duty before he interfered himself. In the result the church did respond to his exhortation, the offender was excommunicated by the majority, he accepted his discipline, he repented, he was restored.

With us today a very different rule generally obtains. If a serious offence is committed, the foreign priest in charge of the district, with or without the assistance of a local committee, inquires into the case; he reports to the bishop. The bishop either hears the case or accepts the report, excommunicates, and issues a sentence which is published in the church. But the church in which the offender lives feels little or no responsibility, and the man is not excommunicated by the majority. Consequently the act has little effect. It does not come home to the offender; it does not come home to the church. A man can afford to present a stubborn front to the fulminations of a foreigner, who is perhaps only an occasional visitor and is always a foreigner.

[1] 1 Cor. 7. 3–5.

He cannot so treat the excommunication of his neighbours.

We look upon the sting of excommunication as exclusion from spiritual privileges; but the man who so acts as to incur excommunication is often the last person to feel that sting. His spiritual apprehension has already been deadened before he falls into sin. What he needs is the public censure of the majority of his fellow-churchmen to awaken his conscience. If the majority of his fellow-churchmen do not avoid him and cast him out, it is little use for a formal sentence of exclusion from church privileges to be issued against him and carried out by the officials of the society alone. That does no good; it very often only does harm. It hardens the man without humbling or instructing him.

Moreover, an act of this kind is done not only for the good of the offender, but for the good of the church. It is meant to clear the church's good name which has been sullied by the act of one of its members. It is meant to be a real clearance of the church. But if the majority feel that they have not a real share in the action of the church, if they do not heartily and sincerely realize that the act is their own act, if they consequently do not support it, then there is no real clearance of the church. Nominally the man is excommunicate, nominally the church has repudiated his act, nominally it has cleared its good name; but if, in fact, this has only been the act of a few officials, then in reality there is no clearance. Christians and heathen alike recognize that the leaders of the church have expressed their disapproval. Christians and heathen alike recognize that the body has done nothing of the kind.

In this case at Corinth we see St Paul's principle of mutual responsibility again enforced, and he enforced it by staying away from Corinth until the church had realized and executed its duty, and had cleared itself of complicity in the crime of this offender. The difficulty with us is that we cannot appreciate this doctrine of mutual responsibility. If a member of a church commits a serious offence we cannot hold the church responsible for his action. We are so individualistic that we cannot understand the practical meaning of St Paul's doctrine of the body and the members. Mystically we accept it; but when it is a question of a single man's crime we ourselves cannot realize, and we cannot bring home to others, their real unity. To punish the society for the offence of the one would seem to us almost unjust. But Eastern people more easily appreciate the corporate aspect of life. To them St Paul's action would not appear at all strange. A Chinese church would not be surprised if the Apostle upbraided them with complicity if they failed to excommunicate an offender. But of course it is quite impossible to exercise any real discipline unless the common conscience of the church is really injured by the offence. That conscience needs to be quickened. By throwing the responsibility on the majority, St Paul stirred and educated the conscience of the whole Corinthian church. If he had sent a letter of excommunication to the elders, and the elders had read it in the church, none of those effects would have followed.

Thus his exercise of discipline was in exact accord with his exercise of authority. Just as he appealed to the corporate conscience to check serious and growing evils in the church, arguing and pleading that the Holy Spirit might enlighten and strengthen his converts; setting forth the principles, persuaded that the Holy Spirit in them would show them how to apply the principles and strengthen them to use them; so in discipline he showed them the right way, but left them to discover how to walk in it. He told them what they ought to do, but not in detail. He threw upon them the responsibility and trusted to them to learn in what way it was to be fulfilled. In the last resort he threatened to intervene, if they refused to do their duty, but it was only after he had exercised all his powers to make his intervention unnecessary.

Therefore he succeeded through failure where we often fail through succeeding. We exercise discipline and leave the church undisciplined. He disciplined the church; we discipline individuals. He left the church, and it stood, tottering on its feet, but still standing; we leave the church without any power of standing at all.

How different would be the action of a modern missionary in dealing with such a state of affairs as that which St Paul encountered at Corinth. His first action, when he discovered the real state of the case, would be to remove the priest in charge as incapable and to substitute another with orders to deal personally with the individual offenders. The errors would be corrected by authority, but the principles would remain unknown and untaught.

I know that someone will say that this is an absurd comparison, that our Eastern converts are infants, and that to talk about principles and to leave the people to find out how to apply them would be to court disaster. But this argument, so convenient for the masterful man, is not really so powerful as it appears. The Easterns are not such infants. They are people who can understand principles. They understand corporate responsibility, in many ways better than we do. Or even if they are infants, infants can only be taught truly by exercising their infant faculties. Dependence does not train for independence, slavery does not educate men for freedom. Moreover, they have the Holy Ghost to strengthen and to guide them. Christians are not only what they are by nature, they are a Spirit-bearing body. It is not a question merely of our faith in them: it is still more a question of faith in the Holy Ghost. We look too much at our converts as they are by nature: St Paul looked at his converts as they were by grace.

CHAPTER II

Unity

We have seen that St Paul did not set out on his missionary journeys as a solitary prophet, the teacher of a solitary individualistic religion. He was sent forth as the messenger of a Church, to bring men into fellowship with that body. His converts were not simply united one to another by bonds of convenience arising from the fact that they lived in the same place, believed the same doctrine, and thought it would be a mutual assistance to form a society. They were members one of another in virtue of their baptism. Each was united to every other Christian everywhere, by the closest of spiritual ties, communion in the one Spirit. Each was united to all by common rites, participation in the same sacraments. Each was united to all by common dangers and common hopes.

In like manner the churches of which they were members were not separate and independent bodies. They were not independent of the Apostle who was their common founder, they were not independent of one another. In St Paul's mind the province was a unit. So, when his churches were established, he distinctly recognized the unity of the Church in the province. He constantly spoke of the churches of Macedonia, of Achaia, of Galatia, of Syria and Cilicia, of Asia as unities.[1] For the purpose of the collection which he made for the poor saints at Jerusalem, the churches of Macedonia, Achaia, and Galatia were each treated as a separate group, and officers were appointed by each group to act on behalf of the province which they represented in the administration of the collection.

This unity was more than a convenient grouping. The same bonds which united individual Christians one to another united the churches. They were not simply groups of Christians who, for mutual assistance and convenience, banded themselves together in face of a common danger. They were all alike members of a body which existed before they were brought into it. They could not act as if they

---

[1] Macedonia: 2 Cor. 8. 1. Achaia: Rom. 15. 26; 2 Cor. 1. 1; 9. 2. Galatia: Gal. 1. 2; 1 Cor. 16. 1. Syria and Cilicia: Gal. 1. 21; Acts 15. 23, 41. Asia: 1 Cor. 16. 19; Judaea: 1 Thess. 2. 14.

were responsible to themselves alone. 'What,' writes St Paul to the Corinthians in rebuking them for allowing women to speak in the church, 'was it from you that the word of God came forth? or came it to you alone?'[1] Or again, in laying down the rule that women should be veiled in the church, he concludes, 'If any man seemeth to be contentious, we have no such custom, neither the churches of God'.[2] For him the Church was prior to the churches. The churches did not make up the Church, but the Church established the churches.

We have seen that St Paul established his churches at centres of Greek and Roman civilization and that they were bound to one another by great trade routes. They were consequently in frequent communication one with another. Visitors passed easily from one to another and prophets soon began to spend their lives journeying from place to place preaching and expounding the faith. The evidence of this frequent communication is abundant. It is quite clear that not only St Paul's own converts, but emissaries from Jerusalem were constantly passing from church to church. It would seem that there was a regular system of commendation by letter,[3] and that anyone who was recognized as a baptized person was welcomed and entertained. Thus the churches were, in fact, united by many bonds of personal interest.

But they were not united only by bonds of personal interest. As the individual converts, as the city churches, so the provincial churches were united by the most real of all bonds, spiritual communion. They were all members of one body. That body was a visible Church liable to all kinds of attacks from very visible enemies. It was held together, not merely by convenience, not merely by common faith, and common sacraments, but also by common submission to a common founder. The unity of the churches in the different provinces was expressed not only in constant intercourse one with another, but by their common recognition of the Apostle's authority as the messenger of Christ to them.

Furthermore, the churches in the Four Provinces were not independent of churches of which St Paul was not the founder. The 'churches of God in Judea' were in Christ before them. St Paul had

[1] 1 Cor. 14. 36.
[2] 1 Cor. 11. 16.
[3] 2 Cor. 3. 1.

been sent forth by the Church in Syria. The churches in the Four Provinces were united to them. The same bonds which made converts members of Christ made them members of the Church; and the Church was not the church in their city only. The same bonds which united the churches in the Four Provinces one to another united the churches everywhere one to another.

St Paul began with unity. In his view the unity of the Church was not something to be created, but something which already existed and was to be maintained. Churches were not independent unities: they were extensions of an already existing unity. There could be no such thing as two churches in the same place both holding the Head, yet not in communion one with another. There could be no such thing as two churches in different places both holding the Head, yet not in communion one with another. There could be no such thing as a Christian baptized into Christ Jesus not in communion with all the other members of the body of which Christ was the Head. If a member was united to the Head he was united to all the other members.

There was a spiritual unity in the one Lord, the one faith, the one baptism, the one God and Father of all. There was an external unity in common participation in common religious rites, common enjoyment of social intercourse. There was no such thing as spiritual unity expressed in outward separation. Spiritual unity is unity, means unity, and is expressed in terms of unity. Outward opposition is a certain sign that spiritual unity does not exist. Spiritual unity in proportion to its perfection and fullness necessarily issues in common, united, harmonious expression, whether of word or act; or else the soul may be God's and the body the Devil's at the same time.

This unity was to be maintained. St Paul wrote much to his churches about unity, but he never spoke of it as of something which they had created. He always spoke of it as a Divine fact to mar which was sin. Unity could be broken. Spiritual pride might express itself in self-assertion, self-assertion might issue in open schism. The Body might be divided. But that was a sin against the Holy Ghost: it was to destroy the temple of the Lord. The act of schism implied and expressed a schismatic, uncharitable spirit. So long as charity had its perfect work, differences of opinion could not issue in schism. The rending of the outward meant the rending of the inward. The separation of Christians meant the dividing of Christ.

That unity might be broken. The dangers by which it was threatened were of the most profound and serious character. The Church began in Jerusalem as a body of Jews who carefully maintained their Jewish tradition and observed the custom of their fathers. The Church in the Four Provinces consisted almost entirely of Gentiles ignorant of that tradition. Consequently, if a Christian from Macedonia or Achaia went up to Judea he must have found himself in a strange atmosphere, in a community as unlike that to which he was accustomed as it is possible to imagine. Circumcision was practised, Sabbaths were kept, meats avoided as unclean, the Law was the practical rule of every-day life. There was a strictness and a reserve which must have oppressed and dismayed him. Christianity in Jerusalem must have seemed to him a thing of rules hardly distinguishable from pure Judaism. Many of the Christians shrank from the Gentile, or tolerated him only as a sort of proselyte. In the meetings of the church the prayers were modelled on Jewish patterns and expressed Jewish thought in Jewish speech with which he was not familiar. The only point of real contact was a common devotion to the Person of Jesus, a common recognition of the same apostles, and a common observance of the same rites of baptism and the Lord's Supper.

On the other hand, when a Christian from Jerusalem went down to Corinth the shock must have been even more severe. The Corinthian in Jerusalem found himself in a society stiff, uncouth, severe, formal, pedantic. The Jewish Christian in Corinth must have thought the church there given over to unbridled licence. Uncircumcised Christians attended the feasts of their pagan friends in heathen temples. Every letter of the ceremonial law was apparently broken every day without rebuke. Even in the meetings of the church, preachings and prayers were built on a strange system of thought which could hardly be called Christian, and there was a most undignified freedom of conduct. He must have welcomed the presence in the church of a party led by men from his own city who argued that in dealing with a people like this it was useless to compromise matters: the only possible course was to enforce the observance of the whole Law throughout the whole Church. To omit anything would simply be to admit the thin end of a wedge which would split Christian morals into fragments. If a man wanted to be saved he must keep the law.

Even amongst themselves the Greeks were not at one. In doctrine and practice there were different schools of thought. Some inclined to maintain that there was some importance in the directions in the Old Testament concerning meats clean and unclean, or in the common conviction that idols were really the instruments by which spirits of superhuman beings came in to intercourse with men and enabled men to approach them with prayers and offerings, or that the disregard of holy days was really a serious offence. Others laughed all these things to scorn, arguing that it was precisely from that kind of religion that Christ had come to set men free, that the Gospel did not depend upon any outward acts or facts. Some went so far as to say that even the Resurrection of the Lord was to be regarded by spiritual men rather as a spiritual than as a material fact, and that if it was apprehended as a spiritual fact in which Christians spiritually shared by faith, then it was not necessary to believe that any actual resurrection of any actual body took place, or if Christ's body rose it was not necessary to conclude that other men's bodies would rise, because spiritually men in virtue of their faith in Christ were already risen.

Thus there was not only a danger of schism in the churches of the Provinces. There was an even greater danger lest the churches of Judea might repudiate and excommunicate the churches of the Four Provinces altogether. To preserve unity under such circumstances was a task of no small difficulty. How then did St Paul overcome this difficulty?

Unity might be maintained in two ways. The Church in Jerusalem might be regarded as the original Church, the body of Christ established and organized by His apostles. The converts in the Four Provinces might be regarded as joining that Church. In that case the new members must be willing to accept the rules and regulations, the laws and the customs of the Society which they joined, and any rebellion against those laws and customs must be treated as an act of schism. The authorities in Jerusalem must be regarded as the final court before which every act of disobedience must be tried. There must be a highly centralized organization. That is the Roman system, a system which has so dominated the modern world that even those who repudiate the papal claims for themselves yet cannot resist the temptation to adopt it in principle when they establish missions among other peoples.

On the other hand, new churches established in the provinces might be regarded equally with the first as parts of a still incomplete whole which must grow up by degrees into its completeness. In this case the new additions would at once be recognized as members of a Spirit-bearing body, equally enjoying the inspiration of the Spirit with the older members. The rules and regulations of the older members of the body could not then be regarded as final and of universal obligation. The first had the customs natural to its own habit of thought designed to satisfy its own needs. The last might equally have its own customs natural to its own habit of thought to meet its own needs. The first had no right, simply on the ground that it was the first, to impose its laws and its customs upon the last. In a word, unity did not consist in outward conformity to the practices of the earliest member, but in incorporation into the body. It would thus be as distinct an act of schism for the earliest to claim a right to dominate the last member as for the last member to assert its own independence of the earlier.

It was the second of these two policies which St Paul adopted. He refused to transplant the law and customs of the Church in Judea into the Four Provinces. He refused to set up any central administrative authority from which the whole Church was to receive directions in the conduct of local affairs. He declined to establish *a priori* tests of orthodoxy which should be applicable for all time, under all circumstances, everywhere. He refused to allow the universal application of particular precedents.

(1) *He refused to transplant the law and the customs of the Church in Judea into the Four Provinces.* For that he went in daily peril of his life, for that he endured calumny, persecution, detraction, for that he risked everything. He himself kept the law, but that availed him nothing. He was pursued from province to province and from city to city by the most cruel and malicious opponents. His work was hindered, his converts perverted, his labours multiplied, his strength worn out. Yet he held on his course; and the establishment of Christianity throughout the then known world was his reward.

(2) *He refused to set up any central administrative authority from which the whole Church was to receive directions.* Once, and once only, he supported an appeal to the Council in Jerusalem to settle a question which arose in another province.[1] The church of that province was

[1] Acts 15. 2.

not of his founding, and it seemed good to the brethren to appeal. But from the Four Provinces there was no such appeal made. When the same or similar difficulties arose in these provinces, he treated these difficulties as questions which each province, if not each church, must settle for itself. He gave his advice and trusted the church to arrive at a right conclusion. When emissaries from Jerusalem attacked him in Jerusalem, he proceeded thither, not to attend a council which might override the provinces, but to maintain the orthodoxy of the provinces and to defend their liberty.

(3) *He declined to establish* a priori *tests of orthodoxy.* We who are eager for such tests, who always want to have it clearly defined beforehand precisely what a church may or may not do, what it may or may not put aside on pain of ceasing to be of the Catholic Church, seek earnestly in the records of the apostolic acts for such a test. And we fail to find it. We know what St Paul taught positively. We have seen how he handed on the tradition and the Scriptures, how he established the orders of the Ministry, how he insisted upon the due administration of the Sacraments. But negatively nothing is defined.[1] It is very strange how difficult it is to find any clear guidance. There was a point beyond which a church could not go without being excluded, just as there was a point of moral conduct beyond which an individual could not transgress without being excommunicated. But as at Corinth the law was not laid down beforehand, as the offences which would necessitate the excommunication of an individual convert were not defined, so the point at which irregular conduct on the part of a church would imply apostasy and would demand exclusion were not defined beforehand.

St Paul never tells us what would happen if something should be done which, as a matter of fact, had not actually been done. His great strength lay in his power to refuse to define, or to anticipate, any heresy or schism. He foresaw that there would be, that there

---

[1] The only definite assertion of such a rule is to be found in Gal. 1. 8. 'Though we, or an angel from heaven, should preach unto you any Gospel other than that which we preached unto you, let him be anathema.' That rule included doctrinal perversions and insistence upon the necessity of a rite which involved a falling from Christ. This case certainly justifies the Church in denouncing heresy when it is manifest and in proclaiming certain practices as destructive of Christian life. But still the statement in the text above is generally true. St Paul did not make a list of opinions or practices which would involve excommunication. He did not even urge the excommunication of Galatian Christians who had submitted to the rite which he denounced as a falling from Christ.

must be, heresy, but he refused to prejudge the matter before the offence was actually committed.

(4) *He refused to allow the universal application of precedents.* When a question had arisen and a judgment had been given he did not apply that judgment as of universal authority. The decrees of the Jerusalem Council were addressed to the churches of Syria and Cilicia. St Paul carried them as far as Galatia,[1] but he carried them no further. He did not enforce them in Macedonia or Achaia. Precedents are not of universal application. The conditions in Corinth or in Thessalonica were not the same as in Antioch in Syria, or even in Galatia. What was vital and natural in Syria would have been artificial in Achaia. It would not have been a precedent to the Corinthians or Thessalonians. It would have been a purely arbitrary ruling. Questions are not settled once for all. They recur in each age and in each country in different forms. They have to be restated and the answer must be revised and restated by the church there on the spot. Nothing is more dangerous than to substitute judgment by precedent for judgment by conviction, and nothing is easier. To appeal to Jerusalem, or Trent, or Lambeth, or Westminster, is easy, but it is disastrous. It makes for an appearance of unity: real unity it destroys. Definitions and precedents have created more schisms than they have healed. If definitions and precedents are dangerous necessities at home, when they are transplanted abroad they become dangerous superfluities. If it is a true doctrine that 'every man must bear his own burden', it is equally true that every age must produce its own definitions and every church its own precedents.

St Paul's conception of unity was so spiritual that it could not possibly be realized by a mere maintenance of uniform practice. It was so spiritual that it could not fail to issue in vital agreement. It was so spiritual that it could not be enforced by compulsion; it was so spiritual that it demanded that it should be expressed in outward unity. The only thing which mattered was the spiritual unity; outward unity which did not express an inward unity was an empty husk. But inward unity was the only thing that mattered, because inward unity which did not express itself in outward unity was the negation of unity.

Hence he laid great stress upon unity.

[1] Acts 16. 4.

(1) *He taught unity by taking it for granted.* He taught men to realize it as a fact of their Christian experience. He taught his converts to recognize every baptized Christian as a brother. He taught them, as we have seen again and again, the duty of mutual responsibility one for another. He taught them by constantly recalling to their minds their common difficulties and sufferings, referring in his letters to the sufferings of other churches and comparing them with their own. He taught them to practise hospitality one to another. At all times, by all means, he kept the fact of the unity of the Church before their eyes.

(2) *He used to the full his position as intermediary between Jew and Greek.* He was a Pharisee with a Greek education and in perfect sympathy with the Greek mind. He carefully kept the law when he was in Jerusalem whilst he strenuously advocated the liberty of the Greeks. He was trusted by all the leaders of the Church and he constantly used that influence. In ten years he went up to Jerusalem three times. After his first journey through Galatia he returned to Antioch and thence went up to Jerusalem for the Council.[1] After the second he considered his presence in Jerusalem of such importance that he refused an urgent entreaty to stay in Ephesus.[2] which was a centre in which he had long designed to preach. At the end of the third journey he insisted upon going up to Jerusalem in spite of earnest and repeated warnings in which he himself believed.[3] The only possible interpretation of this care is that he knew that it was only by his personal intervention that he could hold the churches of Judea and the Four Provinces together and counteract the machinations of the party which would bind upon the Gentiles the burden of the Jewish law, and so either create a schism or destroy his work.

(3) *He maintained unity by initiating and encouraging mutual acts of charity.* The collection for the Jewish saints of Jerusalem was at once a proof and a pledge of unity. It has been universally recognized that St Paul's eager anxiety to secure this collection was due to his sense of the gravity of the situation, and to his conviction that this sign of fellowship in the Gospel would be an immense source of strength to him in the coming struggle with the Judaizing party in Jerusalem. No assurance of orthodoxy in the face of contentious

[1] Acts 15. 2.
[2] Acts 18. 20.
[3] Acts 21. 4; and 10–14.

questions is so powerful as a single act of charity. The real unity which lies at the back of external agreement is common participation in the Spirit of Christ, the spirit of charity. One sign of that Spirit moves men to suppress their grievances and to recognize the rightness of others more than many assertions of orthodox practice. And the influence of the collection is apparent in the refusal of the Church in Jerusalem to take the side of the Judaizing missionaries.

(4) *He encouraged the constant movement of communication between the different churches.* He encouraged his churches in common action for a common end. The collection for the poor saints in Jerusalem was not a series of separate collections made in Galatia, Macedonia, Achaia and Asia, it was a collection made by all these churches together. If it helped to bind the Church in Jerusalem to the churches in the Four Provinces, it also helped to bind the churches in the provinces one to another. They all sent representatives with the Apostle to Jerusalem. When he went up, he went as the head of a large party. It was the presence of a Greek with him in the city which was the immediate cause of the riot. To counteract distorted statements nothing is more valuable than many witnesses. Some may see the worst side of things, but amongst many some will see the best side and the evidence of the many will tend to sound judgment. Hence the value of the growing intercourse between the churches abroad and the Church at home; each helps the other to understand the unity of the Church.

In all these ways St Paul taught his converts to realize the fact of unity.

Today unity is maintained in our missions by a very different means. We have had a long and very bitter experience of schism at home, and all our missions have been planted and organized with the fear of schism ever before our eyes. Our attitude towards our converts is largely the result of this fear, and our methods are largely the offspring of it. We have not established abroad anything that can be compared with the church in the Four Provinces. We have simply transplanted abroad the organization with which we are familiar at home. We have maintained it by supplying a large number of European officials who can carry it on, with the idea that sooner or later we shall have educated the natives to such a point that, if they eventually become the controlling power in the church, the change will be nothing more than a change of personnel. The system will proceed precisely as it did before, natives simply doing exactly what we are now doing. In other words, we have treated unity mainly as a question of organization.

When we establish a mission abroad we make a European the bishop of an enormous diocese, and the diocese is ruled by him essentially in the same way as a diocese is ruled by a bishop at home. He has under him a certain number of white priests who are in charge of districts which they habitually call their parishes, and they govern their parishes on essentially the same principle as the parish priest at home governs his. Externally, there are certain differences. Their flocks are widely scattered, and in consequence priests in charge try to move about as much as they can, and they hold more evangelistic services for those in their parish who are not churchgoers. They have under them priests, deacons, or catechists, who minister to little groups of converts at mission stations larger or smaller, and these stand to them in very much the same relation as curates and lay-readers stand to the parish priest at home. They conduct their services in precisely the same way as their brethren at home. They use the same Prayer Book and the same ritual.

If a traveller returns from visiting our Indian or Chinese Christians the first thing that he tells us is that he was delighted to find himself worshipping in a church where the language indeed was strange and the worshippers of another colour, but that in every other respect he felt quite at home. He found the same sort of ornaments, the same service, the same Prayer Book, the same hymns with which he was familiar. If a Chinese or an Indian convert comes to England he finds, of course, that England is not the Christian country which he imagined it to be, and that the majority of people do not observe many of the rules which he has been taught to keep, but within the circle of the Church he finds the same thing with which he was familiar in his own home. In all the outward forms of religion there is practical uniformity.

There are, of course, divisions, but they are our divisions transplanted into a foreign soil. We have our own parties, and party distinctions are allowed at home and abroad; but there are not divisions between the Church at home and the Church abroad. We import, of course, our own divisions, High and Low, Ritualistic and Anti-ritualistic; but we do not admit the possibility of divergence in manner between East and West. There is nothing that we can really compare with the differences which separated the Church in

Jerusalem from the Church in Corinth or in Ephesus. To find a parallel to our modern missions in the churches of St Paul we should have to imagine a Judaistic church in Macedonia or Achaia divided into Pharisaic, Sadducean, and Grecian parties. In fact, we should have to imagine that St Paul and his fellow-workers were all Judaizers.

No emissaries from Europe or America ever return to accuse some native church of violating the law and the customs. No bishop ever hastens home to claim for the church of his foundation spiritual liberty, and to assert its right to disregard a rubric. None ventures to maintain the equality of one church with another, as equally with it a member of the Spirit-bearing body. A rule is made in London by a Conference of Western bishops and is applied indiscriminately to China and to Africa, and none dares to say that the Chinese have already settled this question for themselves in their own way, and that, though their decision may not approve itself to Englishmen, still it is certainly not a sufficient reason for breaking communion.

With the alteration of a few titles, the same description would, I fear, be equally applicable to the missions of other Christian bodies. They too carry abroad their own organization and forms. They too Judaize in exactly the same way.

The unity, therefore, which we maintain is practically uniformity of custom. It is essentially legal in its habit. When questions arise they are settled by the missionaries, and the missionaries have but one test and that test is agreement with Western practice. If a precedent be found, that precedent settles the question. If a rule of the Western Church, in any way applicable to the case, is to be found, that rule must be followed. If no law, no precedent, seems applicable, some rule or precedent is established which seems most in harmony with the genius and history of the Western Church.

By this means it must be admitted we have succeeded in maintaining a kind of unity. Schism and heresy are almost unknown in our missions. But at what a price have we succeeded! If there has been no heresy, there has been no prophetic zeal. If there has been no schism, there has been no self-realization. If there has been no heresiarch, there has been no Church Father. If there have been no schismatics, there have been no apostles. If there has been no heresy, there has been no native theology. If there has been no schism, there has been no vigorous outburst of life. If there has been no danger of a breach between the New Missions and the Church which founded them, there has been no great advance in the religious life of the Church. The establishment of new churches in the East should bring to us as great a gain as the establishment of Greek churches brought to the Church in the first century. But how can that be, so long as we persist in thinking of the conversion of Eastern people simply as the making of so many proselytes for the communion to which we happen to belong?

PART V

Conclusions

CHAPTER 12

Principles and Spirit

I f we look out over the mission field today we see that we have made most amazing progress, and that our labours have been more than abundantly blessed. We see that we have established all over the world missions through which great numbers of heathen have been brought into the fold of the Church, civilization has been introduced into barbarous countries, immoral customs have been abolished and education and culture have been extended far and wide. On all sides we see steady and increasing progress. It is impossible to have even the most superficial acquaintance with the history and present condition of our foreign missions without being convinced that we have been instruments in the hands of God for the accomplishment of his Divine purpose to sum up all things in Christ.

Nevertheless, there are everywhere three very disquieting symptoms:

(1) *Everywhere Christianity is still an exotic.* We have not yet succeeded in so planting it in any heathen land that it has become indigenous. If there is one doubtful exception to that rule, it is a country where from the very beginning Pauline methods were followed more closely than elsewhere. But generally speaking it still remains true that Christianity in the lands of our missions is still a foreign religion. It has not yet really taken root in the country.

(2) *Everywhere our missions are dependent.* They look to us for leaders, for instructors, for rulers. They have as yet shown little sign of being able to supply their own needs. Day by day and year by year there comes to us an unceasing appeal for men and money for the same missions to which we have been supplying men and money for the last fifty or sixty years, and there seems at present little hope that that demand will change its character. If we do not send men and money the missions will fail, the converts will fall away, ground painfully won will be lost: that is what we are told. When the day comes in which the demand is for men and money to etablish new missions in new country, because the old are capable of standing

alone, the end of our work will be in sight. But at present that day still seems far distant.

(3) *Everywhere we see the same types.* Our missions are in different countries amongst people of the most diverse characteristics, but all bear a most astonishing resemblance one to another. If we read the history of a mission in China we have only to change a few names and the same history will serve as the history of a mission in Zululand. There has been no new revelation. There has been no new discovery of new aspects of the Gospel, no new unfolding of new forms of Christian life.

These symptoms cannot but cause us grave anxiety. There was a day when we rather expected these effects to follow our preaching, and rather prided ourselves upon the fact that no strange elements had produced new and perhaps perplexing developments of Christian thought and life. But today we are living in an atmosphere of expectation. We look forward to new and startling forms of progress. We begin to think that signs of dependent uniformity are signs, not of success, but of failure. We desire to see Christianity established in foreign climes putting on a foreign dress and developing new forms of glory and of beauty. So far then as we see our missions exotic, dependent, uniform, we begin to accuse ourselves of failure.

The causes of that failure are not far to seek.

1. We have allowed racial and religious pride to direct our attitude towards those whom we have been wont to call 'poor heathen'. We have approached them as superior beings, moved by charity to impart of our wealth to destitute and perishing souls. We have used that argument at home to wring grudging and pitiful doles for the propagation of our faith, and abroad we have adopted that attitude as missionaries of a superior religion. We have not learnt the lesson that it is not for our righteousness that we have been entrusted with the Gospel, but that we may be instruments in God's hands for revealing the universal salvation of His Son in all the world. We have not learnt that as Christians we exist by the Spirit of Him who gave up the glory of Heaven in order to pour out His life for the redemption of the world. We have not learnt the lesson that our own hope, our own salvation, our own glory, lie in the completion of the Temple of the Lord. We have not understood that the members of the Body of Christ are scattered in all lands, and that we, without them, are not made perfect. We have thought of the Temple of the

Lord as complete in us, of the Body of Christ as consisting of us, and we have thought of the conversion of the heathen as the extension of the body of which we are the members. Consequently we have preached the Gospel from the point of view of the wealthy man who casts a mite into the lap of a beggar, rather than from the point of view of the husbandman who casts his seed into the earth, knowing that his own life and the lives of all connected with him depend upon the crop which will result from his labour.

Approaching them in that spirit, we have desired to help them. We have been anxious to do something for them. And we have done much. We have done everything for them. We have taught them, baptized them, shepherded them. We have managed their funds, ordered their services, built their churches, provided their teachers. We have nursed them, fed them, doctored them. We have trained them, and have even ordained some of them. We have done everything for them except acknowledge any equality. We have done everything for them, but very little with them. We have done everything for them except give place to them. We have treated them as 'dear children', but not as 'brethren'.

This attitude of mind is apparent everywhere, but it shows itself most distinctly when it is proposed that we should submit any of our actions to the judgment of the native councils which we have established as a training ground for independence. The moment it is suggested that a council in which natives are in a majority should have the power to direct the action of a white missionary, the moment it is suggested that a native, even though he may be a man of the highest devotion and intellectual ability, should be put into a position of authority in a province where white men still hold office, the white missionaries revolt. They will not hear of such a thing. We acknowledge that the Spirit of God has fitted the man for a position of authority, but he cannot occupy it because we are there.[1]

2. Want of faith has made us fear and distrust native independence. We have imagined ourselves to be, and we have acted so as to become, indispensable. In everything we have taught our converts to turn to us, to accept our guidance. We have asked nothing from them but obedience. We have educated our converts to put us in the place of Christ. We believe that it is the Holy Spirit of Christ which

[1] In the last fifteen years there are welcome signs of change in this attitude; but it is still widespread and deep-rooted. (Written 1927.)

inspires and guides us: we cannot believe that the same Spirit will guide and inspire them. We believe that the Holy Spirit has taught us and is teaching us true conceptions of morality, doctrine, ritual: we cannot believe that the same Spirit will teach them.

The consequence is that we view any independent action on the part of our new converts with anxiety and fear. Long experience of difficulties, dangers, heresies, parties, schisms, has made us over-cautious and has undermined our faith in the power of the Holy Ghost. We see the waves boisterous and we are afraid. If anyone suggests giving to the natives any freedom of action the first thought that arises in our minds is not one of eager interest to see how they will act, but one of anxious questioning; if we allow that, how shall we prevent some horrible disaster, how shall we avoid some danger, how shall we provide safeguards against some possible mistake? Our attitude in such cases is naturally negative.

This is why we are so anxious to import the law and the customs. This is why we set up constitutions containing all sorts of elaborate precautions against possible mistakes. We sometimes hope to educate the native in self-government by establishing councils, or synods, on which they are represented, but we hasten to take every possible precaution to avoid the possibility of their making any mistake or taking any action, even in the smallest matters of ritual or practice, which may be contrary to our ideas of what is proper. In the councils we give an overruling authority to the foreign priest: in conferences we make provision for dividing by orders on any question about which the foreigners feel keenly. By all means we try to secure that the real authority and responsibility shall remain in our own hands. We are so familiar with difficulties that we make elaborate preparation to meet every conceivable kind of difficulty and friction before it arises. In so doing we often prepare the way for a difficulty which would never arise if we did not open the door for it to enter. The natives see this and resent it. They see the preparation for over-ruling them, they see that only when they advise what the foreigner approves will their advice be accepted, and they say, 'It does not matter what we think or say; if we suggest anything which the foreigners do not like, all the power is in their hands, and they will do as they please'. So, even when there is perfect agreement, there is no real harmony; and even when the advice of the native representatives is followed, they feel no responsibility for the consequences. It is surprising how carefully the native Christians will consider a question, how eagerly they will seek the advice of their teacher, how willingly they will listen to his suggestions when once they realize that he really trusts them to do what is right, and really intends to let them go their own way even against his own judgment. It is sad how sullenly they will do what they themselves really approve and would naturally do themselves of their own accord, when they think that they are being commanded. It is most sad when they do nothing, because they feel that they have no responsibility. It would be better, far better, that our converts should make many mistakes, and fall into many errors, and commit many offences, than that their sense of responsibility should be undermined. The Holy Ghost is given to Christians that He may guide them, and that they may learn His power to guide them, not that they may be stupidly obedient to the voice of authority.

Moreover, the systems which we import are systems which we acknowledge to be full of imperfections, the sources of many difficulties and dangers at home. We bind on the new converts a burden heavy and grievous to be borne, a burden which neither we nor our fathers were able to bear;[1] and we bind it upon a people who have not inherited it. To us the burden is in a sense natural, it is the result of our own mistakes and sins. We know its history. It has grown upon us. It belongs to us. It is our own. But it is not our converts' in other lands. They do not know its history, nor is it fitted to their shoulders. They will doubtless make their own mistakes. They will create their own burdens; but they need not be laden with ours.

In so acting we have adopted a false method of education. Slavery is not the best training for liberty. It is only by exercise that powers grow. To do things for people does not train them to do them for themselves. We are learning more and more in things educational that the first duty of the teacher is not to solve all difficulties for the pupil, and to present him with the ready-made answer, but to awaken a spirit, to teach the pupil to realize his own powers, by setting before him difficulties, and showing him how to approach and overcome them. The work of the missionary is education in this sense: it is the use of means to reveal to his converts a spiritual power which they actually possess and of which they are dimly conscious. As the converts exercise that power, as they yield themselves to the

---

[1] E.g. we insist upon paid clergy.

indwelling Spirit, they discover the greatness of the power and the grace of the Spirit, and in so doing they reveal it to their teacher. But we are like teachers who cannot resist telling their pupils the answer the moment a difficulty arises. We still live in the age of *Mangnall's Questions*. We cannot resist the temptation to do for them whatever we can do for them. We cannot sit by and see things done ill, or ill in view of our ideas of well. That may be a form of government, but it is not education. The work of the missionary cannot be done by imposing things from without. The one result which he desires is the growth and manifestation of a Spirit from within.

We sometimes acknowledge this, but we excuse ourselves by saying that it is inevitable. We adopt a curious theory about missionary work. We argue that there are three stages of missionary work. In the first the missionary must proceed by introducing the system in which he has been educated, because he must have a system, and that is the only possible system for him. In this stage the missionary must do everything for his converts, because they are infants incapable of doing anything for themselves. Then there is a second stage in which the converts educated in the missionaries' system learn to understand and practise it. Finally, there is a stage in which they may conceivably modify it. With regard to this theory it must be said that as a theory it is untrue, and in practice it is pernicious. In fact there is no such first stage. There is no stage in which converts cannot do anything for themselves. There is no stage in which it is necessary that they should be slaves of a foreign system. The moment they are baptized they are the Temple of the Holy Ghost, and the Holy Ghost is power. They are not so incapable as we suppose.

It is often said that the people to whom we go lack initiative and moral force, that they cannot and will not do anything for themselves, and consequently that, in the early stages, it is absolutely necessary to provide everything for them and to govern them until they acquire a character capable of meeting their own problems. Bu some of the people of whom this is said are seen every day to be capable of carrying on great commercial enterprises. They do not really lack initiative; and if they did, as Christians they should begin to find it. The Spirit of Christ is the spirit of initiative. If they had no initiative without Christ, with Christ they should not fail to have it. That power is in them by the gift of the Holy Ghost. It should be jealously guarded and hopefully encouraged to find larger and larger fields for its activity. But it often fails to find its proper sphere; it is checked and discouraged and stifled in a system in which everything is done under foreign direction. It is exactly because we believe in that power of the Lord that we go. It is the revelation of that Spirit that we seek. To deny it is to deny our hope, to check it is to hinder the attainment of our end.

Again, it is said that we are not now living in the first age of the Church's history, that we cannot go back and act as though these twenty centuries had not been, that we cannot and ought not to rob the new churches of today of the experience of the past, of all that we have learnt by centuries of struggle and labour. That is true. We cannot teach less than the full truth which we have so learnt. But to introduce the fully developed systems in which that truth has expressed itself amongst us is to attempt to ignore differences of race and clime and to omit necessary stages of growth. It is impossible to skip stages of growth. Scientists tell us that each human embryo passes through all the stages by which man has been evolved from lower forms of life. It passes through them, but it now passes through them quickly. In a few months it repeats the history of ages. So our new churches guided and helped might speedily and painlessly learn the lessons which the Church of old learnt with the pain and labour of centuries. But it is one thing to pass through stages quickly, it is another to try to omit them.

Again it is said that methods must change with the age. The Apostle's methods were suited to his age, our methods are suited to ours. I have already suggested that unless we are prepared to drag down St Paul from his high position as the great Apostle of the Gentiles, we must allow to his methods a certain character of universality, and now I venture to urge that, since the Apostle, no other has discovered or practised methods for the propagation of the Gospel better than his or more suitable to the circumstances of our day. It would be difficult to find any better model than the Apostle in the work of establishing new churches. At any rate this much is certain, that the Apostle's methods succeeded exactly where ours have failed.

But, important as I believe it to be in the very early stages of our missions to follow the apostolic practice, which manifestly and un-deniably conduced to his astounding success, yet it is of comparably greater importance that we should endeavour to appreciate the principles in which the Apostle's practice was rooted, and to learn the spirit which made their application both possible and fruitful. Those principles are assuredly applicable to every stage of the Church's growth and that spirit is the Divine spark which should inspire every form of method in order to make it a means of grace. It is scarcely possible to imagine the Apostle in other countries or in another age using a different method; it is quite impossible to imagine him inspired by a different spirit, or adopting other principles of action.

The principles which seem to underlie all the Apostle's practice were two: (1) that he was a preacher of Gospel, not of law, and (2) that he must retire from his converts to give place for Christ. The spirit in which he was able to do this was the spirit of faith.

1. *St Paul was a preacher of a Gospel, not of a law.* His Epistles are full of this. He reiterates it again and again. It was not simply that he was a preacher of a Gospel in contradistinction to the preachers of the Jewish law, he was a preacher of Gospel as opposed to the system of law. He lived in a dispensation of Gospel as opposed to a dispensation of law. He administered a Gospel, not a law. His method was a method of Gospel, not a method of law.

This is the most distinctive mark of Pauline Christianity. This is what separates his doctrine from all other systems of religion. He did not come merely to teach a higher truth, or a finer morality than those who preceded him. He came to administer a spirit. Before St Paul many teachers had inculcated lofty principles of conduct and had expounded profound doctrines. Men did not need another. They needed life. Christ came to give that life, and St Paul came as the minister of Christ, to lead men to Christ who is the life, that in Him they might find life. His gospel was a gospel of power.

So he taught, and for that all his life was one long martyrdom. If he would have admitted for a moment that his work was to introduce a higher law, a new system, he would have made peace with the Judaizers and he would have been at one with all contemporary reformers; but the Gospel would have perished in his hands. In his own words he would have fallen away from grace; Christ would have profited him nothing. That he refused to do and for that he suffered. Men called him an antinomian in consequence; but he was not.

We have seen this truth illustrated in his practice again and again.

148

He did not establish a constitution, he inculcated principles. He did not introduce any practice to be received on his own or any human authority, he strove to make his converts realize and understand its relation to Christ. He always aimed at convincing their minds and stirring their consciences. He never sought to enforce their obedience by decree; he always strove to win their heartfelt approval and their intelligent co-operation. He never proceeded by command, but always by persuasion. He never did things for them, he always left them to do things for themselves. He set them an example according to the mind of Christ, and he was persuaded that the Spirit of Christ in them would teach them to approve that example and inspire them to follow it.

2. *He practised retirement, not merely by constraint, but willingly.* He gave place for Christ. He was always glad when his converts could progress without his aid. He welcomed their liberty. He withheld no gift from them which might enable them to dispense with his presence. He did not speak, as we so often speak, of the gift of orders, or the gift of autonomous government, as the gift of a privilege which might be withheld. He gave as a right to the Spirit-bearing body the powers which duly belong to a Spirit-bearing body. He gave freely, and then he retired from them that they might learn to exercise the powers which they possessed in Christ. He warned them of dangers, but he did not provide an elaborate machinery to prevent them from succumbing to the dangers.

To do this required great faith; and this faith is the spiritual power in which St Paul won his victory. He believed in the Holy Ghost, not merely vaguely as a spiritual Power, but as a Person indwelling his converts. He believed therefore in his converts. He could trust them. He did not trust them because he believed in their natural virtue or intellectual sufficiency. If he had believed in that, his faith must have been sorely shaken. But he believed in the Holy Ghost in them. He believed that Christ was able and willing to keep that which he had committed to Him. He believed that He would perfect His Church, that He would stablish, strengthen, settle his converts. He believed, and acted as if he believed.

It is that faith which we need today. We need to subordinate our methods, our systems, ourselves to that faith. We often speak as if we had to do simply with weak and sinful men. We say that we cannot trust our converts to do this or that, that we cannot commit the truth to men destitute of this or that particular form of education or training. We speak as if we had to do with mere men. We have not to do with mere men; we have to do with the Holy Ghost. What systems, forms, safeguards of every kind cannot do, He can do. When we believe in the Holy Ghost, we shall teach our converts to believe in Him, and when they believe in Him they will be able to face all difficulties and dangers. They will justify our faith. The Holy Ghost will justify our faith in Him. 'This is the Victory which overcometh the world, even our faith.'

CHAPTER 13

Application

The question may well be asked, How far is it possible to follow today the Apostle's methods which I have tried to set forth in the preceding chapters? It is plain that our Missions have hitherto proceeded on very different lines. Is it possible then to make any useful deductions? Is it possible to introduce into our Missions any of these methods without destroying to the very foundations all that we have hitherto established?

We have seen that the secret of the Apostle's success in founding churches lay in the observance of principles which we can reduce to rules of practice in some such form as this.

(1) All teaching to be permanent must be intelligible and so capable of being grasped and understood that those who have once received it can retain it, use it, and hand it on. The test of all teaching is practice. Nothing should be taught which cannot be so grasped and used.

(2) All organization in like manner must be of such a character that it can be understood and maintained. It must be an organization of which the people see the necessity: it must be an organization which they can and will support. It must not be so elaborate or so costly that small and infant communities cannot supply the funds necessary for its maintenance. The test of all organizations is naturalness and permanence. Nothing should be established as part of the ordinary church life of the people which they cannot understand and carry on.

(3) All financial arrangements made for the ordinary life and existence of the church should be such that the people themselves can and will control and manage their own business independently of any foreign subsidies. The management of all local funds should be entirely in the hands of the local church which should raise and use their own funds for their own purposes that they may be neither pauperized nor dependent on the dictation of any foreign society.

(4) A sense of mutual responsibility of all the Christians one for another should be carefully inculcated and practised. The whole community is responsible for the proper administration of baptism, ordination and discipline.

(5) Authority to exercise spiritual gifts should be given freely and at once. Nothing should be withheld which may strengthen the life of the church, still less should anything be withheld which is necessary for its spiritual sustenance. The liberty to enjoy such gifts is not a privilege which

may be withheld but a right which must be acknowledged. The test of preparedness to receive the authority is the capacity to receive the grace.

We have seen further that the power in which St Paul was able to act with such boldness was the spirit of faith. Faith, not in the natural capacities of his converts, but in the power of the Holy Ghost in them.

Now if we are to practise any methods approaching to the Pauline methods in power and directness, it is absolutely necessary that we should first have this faith, this Spirit. Without faith—faith in the Holy Ghost, faith in the Holy Ghost in our converts—we can do nothing. We cannot possibly act as the Apostle acted until we recover this faith. Without it we shall be unable to recognize the grace of the Holy Spirit in our converts, we shall never trust them, we shall never inspire in them confidence in the power of the Holy Spirit in themselves. If we have no faith in the power of the Holy Spirit in them, they will not learn to have faith in the power of the Holy Spirit in themselves. We cannot trust them, and they cannot be worthy of trust; and trust, the trust which begets trustworthiness, is the one essential for any success in the Pauline method.

But if we make that great venture of faith then the application of the Pauline method is still beset with difficulties because the past history of our converts is, as I have pointed out, very different from the history of his converts. Most missionaries today find themselves in charge of mission stations in the midst of established communities of Christians with often a long tradition of foreign government and foreign support behind them. Those communities will probably look to the missionary in everything. He is assisted by a number of native clergy, catechists and teachers whose work it is his duty to superintend. These again will look to him for guidance and encouragement, and probably for definite and particular orders in every conceivable circumstance that may arise, even if they do not depend upon his initiative and inspiration to save them from stagnation. In the central station he will almost certainly find a considerable organization and elaborate establishment which the native Christian community has not created and cannot at present support without financial aid from abroad. He will find that they have been more or less crammed with a complete system of theological and ecclesiastical doctrines which they have not been able to digest. He will find an elaborate system of finance which makes him in the last resort responsible for the raising and administration of all funds in his district. He will find that as regards baptism, the recommendation of candidates for office in the church, and the exercise of discipline, the whole burden of responsibility is laid upon his shoulders alone. He will find in a word that he is expected to act as an almost uncontrolled autocrat subject only to the admonitions of his bishop or the directions of a committee of white men.

He cannot possibly ignore that situation. He cannot act as if the Christian community over which he is called to preside had had another history. He cannot desert them and run away to some untouched field. He cannot begin all over again.

Nevertheless, if he has the Spirit of St Paul he can in a very real sense practise the method of St Paul in its nature, if not in its form. He cannot undo the past, but he can amend the present. He can keep ever before his mind the truth that he is there to prepare the way for the retirement of the foreign missionary. He can live his life amongst his people and deal with them *as though he would have no successor*. He should remember that he is the least permanent element in the church. He may fall sick and go home, or he may die, or he may be called elsewhere. He disappears, the church remains. The native Christians are the permanent element. The permanence of the church depends upon them. Therefore, it is of vital importance that if he is removed they should be able to carry on the work, as if he were present. He cannot rely, and he ought not to rely, upon having any successor. In many cases it must be literally true that he has none, at any rate, for some years. The supply of men from home is happily so inadequate that it is impossible to ensure a sufficient number of European recruits to man all the existing stations. It is obvious that there will not be, and ought not to be, enough to man similar stations all over any great country. In some cases it is probable that he will have no successor: in every case it is desirable that no successor should be necessary to the existence of the church.[1] Consequently, it is of the first importance that he should keep this always before him and strive by all means to secure that the absence of a

[1] This is what gives its peculiar sadness to the recurring appeals of our bishops for men to superintend missions which have been founded for many years. They are appeals not for a cure, but for a palliative. They are simply attempts to put off the evil day. There is in them no recognition of the evil, no resolve to meet and to overcome it, but only a desire to escape from it. The appeal today is the prophecy of another appeal a few years hence.

foreign superintendent should not result in that deplorable lapse from Christianity which we have only too often observed, with shame and grief, to follow upon the withdrawal of foreign support in the past. It is his first duty to prepare the way for the safe retirement of the foreign missionary.

He can do this in two ways: (1) He can associate the people with himself in all that he does and so make them thoroughly understand the nature of the work, and (2) he can practise retirement.

(1) *He can associate the people with himself in all that he does.* He need not do anything without their co-operation. By that I mean not merely that he can associate with himself a few individuals who seem suited to his mind, but that he can educate the whole congregation. In the past we have associated with ourselves individuals of our own selection, we have begun our education from the top. What is needful is to begin from the bottom. Leaders must be thrown up by the community, not dragged up by the missionary. It is necessary to make the whole body realize its unity and common responsibility. It is essential that he should not allow, he certainly must not encourage, the whole body to abandon all its responsibility to others, as he certainly will do if he deals only with a few people whom he has selected. He may avoid this danger by referring all business to the whole congregation in the first instance. In this way he will not only force the whole congregation to understand its responsibility, he will also compel those who are naturally leaders to understand that just as he cannot act as an autocrat because he has been put over them by the bishop, so neither can they so act because they have attracted his attention by some display of intellectual or social superiority. It is essential that the whole body should grow together. Now in doing this we shall find that the missionary must, in fact, follow the example of St Paul very nearly, as we shall see if we take a few instances. Let us take four typical examples of the Pauline method: the management of funds, the administration of baptism, the selection of ministers for the congregation, the exercise of discipline.

(a) *Finance*. It is important that the missionary should educate the whole congregation in the principles of church finance because this is a question which touches every member directly in a very obvious way, and when the people learn to understand that the control of finance is in their own hands they will more easily and quickly learn their responsibility in other matters. Even where, as in some central stations, a considerable proportion of the annual income is derived from foreign sources we need not hesitate to take this course. The missionary can teach the congregation as a congregation the sources from which all money is derived. He can make them understand what money is wanted and why it is wanted. He can generally give them control of all local expenses. He need not take charge of any money collected by the congregation even at their instant and special desire. He can refuse to accept the administration of money for which he is wholly and solely responsible. The modern institution of church councils will greatly assist him in this, but in the actual administration of money in small communities he need not even use a council. He can easily teach the whole community; for finance is a subject in which the whole congregation is naturally interested. If the people appoint a council to administer local funds, the council may be responsible to them primarily, and the use and abuse of funds may still be really in their hands. Only here is it unfortunately necessary to remark that it is no use to pretend. To consult the people whilst the missionary intends to carry out his own plans to hand over money to them and to keep control over it at the same time, is fatal. The people at once see the deception and resent it. They must be allowed to learn by making their own mistakes.

Of all local finance the administration of charity is the simplest and most instructive. The relief of distress should be entirely in the hands of the congregation. The creation of a charity committee is not so good an educational method in a small community as is the alleviation of individual cases as they arise by the whole congregation. Cases of poverty may be referred at once to the whole congregation. Everybody knows everybody else. The congregation knows exactly what is needed. They can reject the appeal or subscribe to meet it on the spot. The missionary, if he will, may subscribe with the others. Nothing is more calculated to draw the congregation together and to help the people to realize their mutual dependence, than the supply of special needs by special acts of charity one towards another. A poor fund, if it is administered by a missionary, only tends to misunderstanding and discontent.

Even in such matters as the foundation of schools, the congregation ought to manage its own business. The first thing is to persuade the people of the need for a school. Until they desire it and are ready to support it, nothing is done. When they want it, they will certainly seek the missionary's help. He can give help, why should he insist upon control? He and they, they and he, should think out the plans, seek for sources of supply, and engage the teacher. It is essential that the people should recognize that the school is their own school, not simply his. If he does the work for them, even though he may induce them to subscribe, the work will be his work not theirs, and they will feel no responsibility for its success or failure.[1]

Similarly, if a school is to be enlarged the missionary has another opportunity of teaching his people the same lesson. The school is really their school, not his, even if it has been founded in the first instance with foreign money. It is their children who are to be educated in it. They are really more nearly affected by the alteration than we are. Then they should be consulted, and their advice should be taken. It is a grievous loss to the whole Church if the work is done simply by foreigners, when the whole community might be made to realize, as perhaps they never realized before, its importance to them and their responsibility for it.

In finance, as in other matters, the principle of throwing upon the shoulders of the native Christians all the responsibility that they can carry, and more than they can carry, is a sound one. If they have more than they can manage, they will gladly seek advice and help; if they have less, they will, sooner or later, begin to fight for more or to feel aggrieved that they are not given their proper place.

(b) *Baptism.* The admission of new converts is a matter which very intimately affects the whole Church. It cannot but seriously affect

[1] There is one aspect of this question which I can only refer to with grief and shame, but I dare not omit it. I am afraid that there are congregations who have been so ill-educated by us in the past that they would be ready to sell themselves to the highest bidder. If they were free, and thought that they could get larger grants from another mission, they would go over. If they wanted help to build or enlarge schools more than their own missionary could supply, they would threaten to accept help from some other society. And I fear that there are Christian missions which would offer them such help for the sake of augmenting their numbers. In such cases we should have to consider carefully whether it was worth while to keep them at the price. They ought to have the case set clearly before them, and obviously it is essential that they should know and feel that the missionary is solely devoted to securing their true welfare. But if they resolve to sell themselves to another Society for a school, they should be prevented from so doing by no other than moral persuasion, and I cannot believe that many congregations would accept the bait held out to them, if they saw that their liberty and self-respect were involved. But, in the last resort, if persuasion fails, I believe that the attempt to retain our hold on congregations of Christians by merely financial bonds is unworthy and futile.

the whole community if improper persons are admitted or proper persons excluded. It is of vital importance that the Christians should learn to recognize this. It is possible to teach them and to help them to feel a proper responsibility in the matter. They will recognize the truth and feel the responsibility, if the truth is taught them and the responsibility is thrown upon them. No convert should be admitted by baptism into the body without the approval of the body, as a body. If a man wishes to be baptized he must be accepted by the congregation. But some one will say, 'If we do that, men will be rejected whom the missionary is convinced are proper persons'. If that is so, then the missionary must try to educate the congregation, but he will do that not by overruling them with a high hand, but by teaching them true principles. If the convert must go to the church, so must the missionary. He must entreat, exhort, advise with all long-suffering. He may fail to obtain his end in a particular case. But the people may be right and he be wrong. Even if he is right, he may really gain more by allowing the people to overrule him than by overruling them. They will speedily see that they are dealing with one who earnestly seeks their welfare, but will not force his own views upon them, and they will certainly be in greater danger of erring through their desire to please him than through their desire to vex him, or even to drive him away.

(c) *The appointment of ministers.* If a man is to be trained at a central school as a catechist or teacher, it is of the first importance that he should feel that he is sent by the whole community, not by the favouritism of a foreign missionary, that he is supported by the common assent and approval, that he represents the body, and that he will be received on his return by the whole body. No missionary is compelled to recommend in such cases on his sole authority. It is not enough that he should consult the Christians, he may see to it that the choice is the real choice of the whole congregation, or group of congregations, to which the candidate belongs. Beyond that the missionary cannot at the present time go. The appointment of catechists, deacons and priests to posts in the diocese is generally in the hands of the bishop or of a committee, and the people to whom the man is sent are seldom, if ever, consulted. So long as this is the case the missionary is compelled to accept the nominee of that committee, and the people can scarcely be expected to understand the true relations between the pastor and his flock. The situation is grievous; but in old-established missions it is at present unavoidable. For no one can expect a committee directed by foreigners to act on Pauline principles. The committee will inevitably make the bonds which bind the native ministers to itself as tight as possible, and the bonds which unite the minister to his flock proportionately weak. But if the missionary sees to it that no candidate is sent up from his district until he has really been selected and approved by the people to whom he naturally belongs he will lay a foundation upon which a better system may one day be established. At any rate, he will remove the common complaint that candidates for ordination and clergy are at the mercy of one man and that to displease the superintending missionary even accidentally is certain to result in the ruin of the man's career.

(*d*) *Discipline.* Cases of moral failure are more simple. In nearly every case the missionary in charge is left a very large discretion in such matters. He can act as St Paul acted. If a man falls into grievous sin, if an offence is committed which ought to shock the conscience of the whole Christian community, he need not deal with it directly. He can call the attention of the congregation to it and point out the dangers manifest and pressing of leaving it unrecognized or unreproved. He can call upon them to decide what ought to be done. He can in the last resort refuse to have any dealings with a congregation which declines to do its duty and tolerates gross open immorality in its midst. He can entreat, exhort, advise, he may even threaten, the whole body when it would be fatal to deal with the individual himself. If he can persuade them to do what is right, the whole community is uplifted; but he cannot put them in the right way by doing for them what they alone can do.[1]

(2) *He can train them for retirement by retiring.* He can retire in two ways, physically or morally. He can retire morally by leaving things more and more in their hands, by avoiding to press his opinion, by refusing to give it lest he should, as is often the case, lead them to accept his opinion simply because it is his. He can retire by educating them to understand all the working of the mission and by gradually delegating it. He can retire physically. He can go away on missionary

---

[1] A missionary in South Africa told me that he had practised the theory of discipline which he first found in this book, and that the result had surprised him. 'For the first time,' he said, 'I felt that we got to the root of the matter and justice was being done.'

tours of longer and longer duration, leaving the whole work of the station to be carried on without any foreign direction for a month or two. He can do this openly and advisedly because he trusts his people. He can prolong his tours. He can find excuses for being away more and more. He can even create such a state of affairs that he may take his furlough without their suffering any harm. At first, no doubt, he would be anxious, and he would have good cause for anxiety. Things would go wrong. But his people would know his mind, and, though they would grudge his absence, they would see that he was really helping them most by leaving them. Retirement of that kind, deliberately prepared and consciously practised, is a very different thing from absence through stress of business unwillingly. Only by retirement can he prepare the way for real independence.

But the difficulty instantly arises that in many cases the retirement of the missionary would mean that the Christians would be deprived of the sacraments. That is too often true, and it is apparently an insuperable difficulty. The only way out of it is to persuade the Bishop to ordain men in every place to celebrate the sacraments. There are plenty of suitable men. Everywhere there are good, honest, sober, grave men respected by their fellows, capable of this office, and they ought to be ordained for that special purpose. But meanwhile, even at the risk of depriving the Christians at the centre of that spiritual food which is their right, the missionary should retire, at any rate for a few months, in order to evangelize new districts, and above all to teach his people to stand alone.

But in every district the missionary has not only to deal with settled congregations. If he is an evangelist he is always beginning work in new towns or villages with new converts. Then he can begin at the very beginning. He can make the rule of practice the rule of all his teaching. Wherever he finds a small community of hearers he can begin by teaching them one simple truth, one prayer, one brief article of the Creed and leaving them to practise it. If on his return he finds that they have learned and practised that first lesson, he can then teach them a little more; but if he finds that they have not succeeded, he can only repeat the first lesson and go away again so that they may master that one before they are burdened with another. If they learn to practise one act alone they may make more progress than if they had learned by heart all the doctrines of the Church and depended solely upon some outside teacher.

He need not take it for granted that, if men are converted, there is no hope for the conversion of their wives and children until he can get women missionaries and teachers to instruct them in the rudiments of the Gospel. He can tell his first converts that they are responsible not only for their own progress, but for the enlightenment of their wives and families and neighbours. In some places the difficulties of this are apparently insuperable; but men overcome apparently insuperable difficulties by the power of the Holy Ghost. We need not take it for granted that men or women must run away from home, or cannot influence their households and teach them what they have learned. It is better to take it for granted that they can, even to the death. Slaves in heathen households in Rome were in apparently an impossible position; yet they overcame the apparent impossibility.

He need not take it for granted that every small community of hearers must have a catechist settled amongst them. Where there are three people one will inevitably lead. On his visits the missionary, or his catechist, can give special attention and teaching to these natural leaders and instruct them to hand on to the others the special teaching which they have received. This can be done if the instruction given is given line upon line, and if there is no haste to complete a theological education. So these leaders will grow with their fellows, with those whom they teach. They will learn more by teaching than in any other way. If the missionary is fortunate he may be able to induce his bishop to ordain some of these men of approved moral character and natural authority. In that case the church in that part will grow naturally into completion: otherwise, his converts will be compelled to wait for his visits to receive the sacraments, the work will be retarded, and the people starved. But even so, he can make them largely independent in all other respects. The visits of the missionary will be welcomed as the visits of a friend who can help them. They will eagerly seek his advice, they will need his encouragement. But *whatever they have learnt, they will have so learnt that they can practise it, even if he never came near them again.* It would be better to teach a few men to call upon the name of the Lord for themselves than to fill a church with people who have given up idolatry, slavishly and unintelligently, and have acquired a habit of thinking that it is the duty of converts to sit and be taught, and to hear prayers read for them in the church by a paid mission agent.

The missionary can observe the rule that no organization should be introduced which the people cannot understand and maintain. He need not begin by establishing buildings, he need not begin by importing foreign books and foreign ornaments of worship. The people can begin as they can with what they have. As they feel the need of organization and external conveniences they will begin to seek about for some way of providing them. The missionary, or his helper, can encourage and assist them. They may even subscribe money, but if they do this, it should be a subscription from them, freely given, and entirely in the control of the little congregation. Their finance so far as they have any common finance may be entirely in their own hands. It will obviously be small, and because it is small it is of great importance that they should learn to manage it themselves, so that they may be prepared to understand the larger finance of a wider area when they begin to find their place in an organization which covers a large district.

Similarly with all church rules, it is not necessary to begin by insisting upon mere verbal assent to a code of law. The new converts may grow up into it. If they learn to pray in twos and threes, if they learn to read as they may be able the Holy Gospels,[1] and to discuss amongst themselves the lessons of the teacher they will gradually perceive the inconsistency of that which they read or hear with heathen practices to which they have been accustomed. They will inquire amongst themselves and dispute; they will refer the question to the missionary on his visit and he will have opportunity of explaining wherein the custom in question is agreeable or otherwise to the doctrine which they have been taught. But he need not hurry them. They must learn to change because they feel the need of change, and to change because they see the rightness of the change, rather than to change because they are told to do so. If they change unintelligently, by order, they will easily relapse, because they have never seen the principle on which the change is based. Artificial changes are not likely to be permanent until they have become in process of years habitual, and then they will still be unintelligent. Changes made under the influence of the Holy Spirit are reasonable, and, so

---

[1] I have seen converts of the lowest castes in India after one year's teaching capable of reading and understanding the Gospels and doing the work of lay evangelists most efficiently.

made, are the accepted changes of the people themselves. From those they can only fall away by deliberate apostasy. So we advance at home. We educate public opinion until that opinion is on the side of righteousness and then the change is permanent. So, e.g., we put down slavery. And so we may deal with our converts.

Our past efforts have not been so fruitless but that we have now a great number of Christians who, beginning by accepting Christian law as an external demand of the foreign teachers, have ended by seeing its true meaning and accepting it as a proper expression of the will of God and here we have a powerful influence and example. New converts will speedily strive to attain the level of their fellows. They will see the manifest advantages. By setting the example before them of Christian communities more advanced than themselves, by encouraging them to take their difficutlies to their more educated brethren, we can encourage and help them without enforcing authoritative, and to them incomprehensible, demands.[1] Some things they will speedily accept because they are true and natural expressions of the mind of Christ in them; some things they will accept only after a long struggle, because they are not easily understood; and some things they will never accept because they are neither natural nor proper expressions of the mind of Christ in their lives; and such things have never been really accepted, even by those who have outwardly submitted to them.

But there would certainly arise cases in which the people would for a long time observe practices which the missionary would be compelled to condemn as superstitious, immoral, or otherwise iniquitous. Still the true method is purely persuasive. The missionary must use his judgment as to whether the refusal is deliberate rejection of a truth which the people know to be truth and will not accept, or whether it is due to ignorance and immature ideas of the nature of Christianity. In the latter case he can go on teaching, exhorting, persuading, certain that so far as he is right, he will lead the people to see that he is right. In the former case, he has no resort but to shake off the dust of his feet, to refuse to teach men who will not be taught. Compulsion is futile, and disastrous. There are men who will be taught. He must seek out those and turn to them.

This applies to all missionary preaching. The one test which the missionary should require of his hearers is openness of mind. If he

[1] The law as regards marriage is a noteworthy example of this.

teaches, he teaches as one who is making a moral demand, and if that moral demand is met with a flat determination to resist it, then he cannot well continue his teaching. Willingness to send children to school in order to obtain material advantage, if coupled with a determination not to submit to the claims of Christ, is not a field in which the doctrine of Christ can be planted. Willingness to listen to the preacher in order to rise in the social scale by becoming Christian is very different. There is a willingness to accept the teaching. The motive is low, but the willingness to accept is present, and the teacher can there plant seeds which will grow up and purify the motive. This has happened again and again. Willingness to hear for the sake of advantage with a determination not to submit to the doctrine is one thing, willingness to hear for the sake of advantage with even a half-hearted intention of accepting the doctrine is another. There must be in the hearers a willingness, not only to hear but to accept, if the missionary is to persevere with success. Everywhere there are those whose hearts God touches and so bring prepared hearts. On those the missionary may concentrate his attention. For them there is hope. Everywhere there are those who refuse to hear with their souls, who close their hearts. These we must prepare to refuse to teach. We must be prepared to shake the lap.

So far, any missionary who chooses can go today, without upsetting the work of his predecessors, but building upon it. Many things may seem desirable, but this at least is possible.

CHAPTER 14

Epilogue

A Present-day Contrast

It may perhaps add point and reality to the argument which I have tried to set forth in the preceding pages, if I illustrate it by examples taken from modern life. I have imagined two men working under fairly similar circumstances. I have first made a composite photograph. All the details are taken from life, but no one missionary supplied me with them all. The picture which results is consequently imaginary; but it will, I think, be at once recognized as representing a real type, and that not an uncommon one. The second illustration is not composite. It is the actual experience of one actual man, and the story is extracted almost verbatim from his diary of his work.

I

The missionary was a good man, devoted to his work. He was sincerely desirous of building up the native church. He laboured in a large district and tried hard to do the work of two or three men.

He began by building schools and churches. He saw that unless the children of his converts received some education, they could not progress as he desired to see them progress. He saw that their parents were poor and could not afford to do very much to promote education; they could hardly afford to lose the help of their children even when they were young. Consequently he was driven to look elsewhere for support. He besought societies, he wrote letters, he enlisted the sympathies of his friends at home, he collected subscriptions. He exhorted and taught his converts until they began to understand that it was to their advantage to lend their help. Moreover they knew that he sought their welfare, and they were inclined to help him in any work which he started. So out of their poverty they subscribed money and labour, and in due course the schools were built—primary schools in the villages, and a high school at the central station. The schools were built on mission property and belonged to the mission, and the mission supplied the teachers, and relied upon the teachers to keep up the interest of the church-folk in them and to induce them to send their children.

Similarly the missionary provided churches for his people. He said that if corporate church life was to be a reality the converts must have churches. These were provided in the same way and entailed no small labour and anxiety. In some cases he actually assisted at the building with his own hands: in all he exercised careful and consistent supervision. He was very anxious that his buildings should be as good and as church-like as possible, and not only in the exterior but in the internal fittings he strove to have everything not only good but attractive and complete. With the help of his friends in England he succeeded in providing some of them with bells and harmoniums. He introduced surpliced choirs, he induced guilds of ladies in England to send him out altar linen and frontals. He instructed his people in the use of the Prayer Book, and he managed by dint of persevering labour to teach them to conduct the service in good order. He even got them to sing translations of *Hymns Ancient and Modern*, for they were a musical people; though the tunes were to them unnatural and the translations imperfect and sometimes, to them, almost incomprehensible. Thus the services in his churches became the admiration of visitors from England.

Yet he was not quite satisfied. Churches and schools alike required perpetual supervision. There was a tendency amongst the converts to let things fall into decay the moment that his inspiring presence was withdrawn for a short time. The surplices were allowed to get dirty and ragged, the altar frontals became moth-eaten, the very fabric of the buildings was neglected. The people inclined sometimes to meet in informal services to sing native hymns which one of them had written to native tunes, to the neglect of the daily offices. The missionary was disheartened. He saw that it would take a long time to establish a habit of decent, orderly service, as he understood it. His converts had subscribed liberally, and he had boasted of their self-support. Yet they did not seem to look upon the fruits of their liberality as their own. They did not show any eager zeal to draw others from their heathen neighbours into the church.

Consequently he welcomed eagerly a diocesan scheme for the establishing of native church councils, because he hoped that, by this means, his people would learn to take a more intelligent and active part in the management of the church. He immediately set to work to carry out the new scheme. He directed his native pastors and helpers to see that the councils were elected. At first neither pastors nor people understood it. They saw in it simply a new method of getting money. One of the native pastors thus described his experience to a stranger: 'The people come to us and they say, "What does this mean? We do not want to be consulted. The missionaries are our father and our mother. Let the missionary tell us what to do and we will do it". And I say, "The missionaries have directed this. They want you to do this. They think it will educate you in the management of affairs and will make you more self-supporting. We must do it."' And they did. By degrees they began to find that it was interesting to be consulted, and they gained a new sense of importance. They not only subscribed money but within certain limits they administered it. It was true that the missionary audited all their accounts and objected strongly to any expenditure that he had not authorized, but, still, under his direction they did administer some funds. They also learnt to criticize the use of funds. They knew that much money came into the missionary's hands from mission sources, and they surmised that he administered more than they knew. They knew how much they themselves gave. They knew that the missionary boasted of their generosity. They, too, began to feel that they were doing a great deal. To strangers their first remark was a modest boast that they were far advanced in self-support, their second was a hint that they did not receive so much out of the mission funds as they thought that they had deserved.

They were not, of course, allowed to go far in self-government. The missionary felt that it would be extremely dangerous if people who had not learnt to walk were allowed to run. All their meetings were of the nature of instructions in what the missionary thought should be done, rather than free proposal and discussion. 'If they did what they liked, what should I do,' said the missionary, 'if they wanted to do something of which I did not approve? I must keep the direction of affairs in my own hands.' In this he was ably supported by his native pastors who were entirely independent of their congregations. The missionary wanted to appoint a special catechist to work amongst children—a sort of special missioner for children. In one pastorate the pastorate committee refused to see the wisdom or necessity of this; but the missionary had expressed a wish for it, and the pastor followed the missionary. The pastorate committee refused to support the plan, so the pastor vetoed their resolution. The district committee sitting under the chairmanship of the missionary accepted the plan. It was carried out. The pastorate committee thereupon passed a resolution to the effect that as the proposal had been carried over their heads and they disapproved of, it, they would not vote any money for its support. The pastor vetoed that resolution also, and paid the money out of the church fund, of which he was treasurer. Nevertheless, in spite of the fact that the committees did not always see eye to eye with their missionary, and consequently had to be overruled, their very existence did encourage the converts in self-support and did teach them the art of self-government to a certain degree. And the missionary was glad of that. He really wanted them to learn to manage their own affairs, only in the early stages he felt that it was of vital importance that they should not be allowed to go wrong.

Similarly in cases of discipline he was most anxious to educate the people. He did not believe in the exercise of discipline as the mere decree of white missionaries. He thought the people should be represented. In cases of serious wrong-doing, he caused a committee of inquiry to be appointed, and if the case presented any peculiar difficulty he himself went down and sat on the committee at the inquiry. No doubt justice was done. But it was disappointing to find that Christians often refused hospitality to a man who had been so excommunicated when the missionary was present, and then received him when the missionary was absent. They did not seem to realize the full responsibility of their action. If it was suggested that the case might have been different if the native body had acted in the first instance alone, the answer was conclusive: 'It would be dreadful if the Native Committee condoned a moral offence.'

Such was the missionary's energy and success in governing his native converts that he was appointed Secretary of the Diocesan Conference of his Mission. There he could exercise his abilities over a wider area. It was unfortunate that his knowledge of the language was not sufficient to enable him to write or translate papers quickly, because the rule of the Conference was that all business should be transacted in the native tongue; but the difficulty was got over by allowing the rule to lapse. Happily nearly all the native members of conference, or at any rate all the more influential members, could speak English, and speeches could be delivered on occasion in the vernacular for the benefit of those who could understand no other tongue. But here, too, the missionary and his fellows felt the necessity of keeping the conduct of affairs safe in their own hands. One day, one of his own people rose at the conference to propose that a certain building which had been originally put up as a residence for a foreign missionary should be converted into a secondary school for the people of that district. This was a proposal of which the missionary heartily disapproved. It struck directly at the position of the secondary school in his own central station which was under his own immediate care. He rose to oppose it. Nevertheless he could not convince the proposer, who again got up and began a long speech on behalf of his plan. He was very eager about it because he was himself a native of the place and a leading churchman there. Thereupon the missionary broke in and cut him short abruptly. His argument, this time was conclusive. 'Well, anyhow,' he said, 'it is *our* building, it is not *your* building, and we will not let you have it for the purpose.'

II

The second was in charge of a much smaller district. He began by approaching his bishop with a request that the usual grant given for the upkeep of his mission station might be withdrawn. He desired that his own salary and the salaries of his three native catechists might be paid them but no more. 'If,' he said, 'we need money for any purpose, we will apply for it, explaining what we can do, what we propose to do, and what help we need, and you, if you think good, can help us out of mission funds. I will see that the work is done, and will inform you when it is done. But I shall keep no mission accounts, for I shall never keep any mission money in my hands.'

At the direction of his bishop, and as part of a diocesan scheme, he caused a council to be elected by the four little churches in his district, and he used that council. If anything needed to be done in any of the churches, either the congregation found out the need for itself, or the missionary suggested the need until the congregation felt it. When they recognized the need, they met as a congregation to discuss it (if the missionary was present, he was present; if he was not, he was not), and to consider what they could do to supply it. If they could supply it, they did so without any further question, and when the missionary came round they displayed their work with pride and were duly congratulated. If they needed help, they instructed their representatives to go to the District Council to appeal for them. The representatives appeared at the council, and set forth the case, and said how much the local church could guarantee towards the expense and how much they needed.

The District Council had a small fund in the hands of its treasurer from which, if it approved of the scheme, it voted a grant. If that was not enough to supply the need, the missionary then reported the matter to the bishop: 'The local church wants *such and such* things done. It is prepared to subscribe *so much*; the District Council is prepared to subscribe *so much*; they still need *so much*. I think the local subscription is sufficient to justify the conclusion that the people really are in earnest about it (or are *not*, as the case might be). I think the District Council grant is sufficient to justify the conclusion that the council is agreed that the work ought (or ought *not*, as the case might be) to be done. Can you supply the deficiency?' If the money was given, it was handed over to the District Council, which then gave it with its own grant to the local church, and the work was done, and there an end.

At first this caused great amazement amongst the people. A local church wanted a school. The people appealed to the missionary and asked him to found one in their village. They said, 'We want a school'. 'Then why don't you get one?' was the answer. They were astonished. 'What?' they said, 'how can we get one?' 'How do your heathen neighbours get their children taught?' 'They subscribe together and invite a teacher.' 'Well, why don't you do that?' 'But that has never been done. The missionary has always found the teacher.' 'I cannot help that. I do not see why I should find your teachers. I have no teachers; you have. Is there not among you a single man who can teach a few little boys to read and write and say their catechism?' 'But *may we* do that?' 'Of course, why not?' 'But how shall we pay him?' 'Look here,' said the missionary, 'you go away and think it out and talk it over. See what you can do and then come and report to me, and perhaps I will give you a subscription out of my own pocket, if you are in difficulties.' (Here he made a mistake; he ought to have told them to report to the District Council: but it was his first case, and he had not himself thought things out.) So they went away, and in due course the school was begun. It cost the missionary about £1.

He said little about the Church, the Body, Unity; he always acted as if the Church, the Body, the Unity was a reality. He treated the church as a church. He declined to treat individual members of the body as mere individuals. Before he reached the district there had been grievous troubles and disturbances, great persecutions, and afflictions. In fear of their lives some of the Christians had fallen away. They did not indeed, so far as I know, practise heathen rites, but they did not come to church and they were unwilling to be openly associated with the Christian congregation. The missionary did not search out these people. He addressed himself to the church. He pointed out to the church the great danger in which these lapsed Christians were, and how serious were the evils which might result from their continued impenitence. He reminded the Christians that they formed the permanent element in the church, and that the good name of the church was of vital importance to them. He asked them what steps they proposed to take, and he left them to decide what they thought ought to be done. They appointed certain of their number to visit the lapsed Christians, in order to set before them the dangers of their state and to ask them to decide on which side they would stand: with the Church for Christ, or with the heathen. They sent out their representatives with prayer. They received their report with thanksgiving. In a few days most of the lapsed were restored to the church.

One case was of a more difficult character. In the height of the persecution a prominent member of the church had driven away his son's wife, and had contracted for him a marriage with the daughter of one of the leaders of the persecuting society. This had happened more than two years before the missionary arrived in the district. For two years the offence had been passed over in silence. The offender and his son were both still Christians in name. As soon as the missionary found this out he called the church together. Again he urged upon the Christians the grievous and palpable dangers of condoning such an offence. Again he left them to consider what ought to be done. After a time the catechist, and one or two other members of the church, came to tell him that the church was agreed that the offenders ought to be excommunicated publicly. To that he replied that it was not within the power of the local church to excommunicate any member. All that they could do was to forward their resolution to the bishop with the request that he would take action in the case. He said that he was quite willing to write to the bishop for the church in that sense. So he did. But in the meanwhile he met the offender and told him what the church was doing. The offender came to see him. He was much disturbed. 'Why,' he said, 'cannot you act as your predecessors have always acted? Before, if any one did anything wrong, the priest wrote a letter to the bishop, the bishop wrote a letter to the church, the letter was read out in church, the man stayed away, and after that no more was said about it. Why cannot you do that? Why do you stir up all the Christians in such matters?' The missionary answered that public notorious offences concerned not only the priest-in-charge and the bishop, but the whole church, and that it was right that the church should act in such cases as a body. 'But what can I do?' asked the man. 'I cannot bear this.' The missionary replied that he did not know, but that he thought that if the man was truly penitent, and made public confession in the church, and then published his confession in the city, so that the name of the church was cleared, then the Christians might be satisfied and that he might remain in the church as a penitent, until the Hand of God made clear the way for his full restoration. Thereupon the man departed. Afterwards the missionary met his catechist and told him what he had said, and asked him whether he thought the Christians would be satisfied with such an act of penitence. 'It is of no importance,' answered the catechist, 'what they think. Such a thing has never been done since the world began. Whatever he may do, he will not do that.' Yet he did. It is one thing to be excommunicated by a foreign bishop, it is quite another to be excommunicated by one's neighbours. The whole church was in a ferment. Many of the Christians were connected by family ties with the offenders. They took the matter seriously to heart. Prayers went up to God night and day from individuals and from the whole church. The offender read out in church a confession couched in the simplest and most definite terms. In it he confessed that he had committed such an offence, that his action was contrary to the laws of God and the Church, that he was persuaded that salvation was to be found in Christ in communion with His Church, and that thenceforward he would endeavour to conform his life to the Law of God. He went out with two or three of the leaders of the church and posted that confession on the four gates of the city.

Soon the missionary learnt that the secret of success in his work lay in dealing with the church as a body. When questions arose he had but one answer, 'Tell it to the church'. A man came to him one day with a long tale of persecution. His landmark, he said, had been removed by a heathen neighbour who, not content with robbing him, was accusing him of the very offence which he himself had committed. The injured Christian begged for assistance against his adversary. The only answer that he received was, 'Tell it to the church'. Eventually he did so. After service one Sunday morning, he rose and said, 'I have business for the church'. All gave him a patient hearing whilst he poured out his tale. Then an old farmer in the congregation rose and asked: 'Has your adversary taken the case into court?' 'No, but he threatens to do so.' 'Then I propose that we adjourn this matter until he carries out his threat.' Not another word was said. Some weeks later the same man came to say that his enemy had now taken the case into court and to appeal for help. Again, an old man arose: 'I think that we had better not consider this matter any more.' Again the sentence was received in silence. In that silence the whole church had condemned their brother. They held him to be in the wrong. A question which might have perplexed and troubled a foreigner, one in which he might easily have made a serious mistake, was settled. No Christian in the congregation would have dared to tell a foreign priest that the man was wrong. None would have dared to advise him not to give his countenance to another. But none was ready to uphold the evil himself, none need break that silence of condemnation. They all knew every detail of the case, details which none would have ventured to utter even in private. The aged, respectable leader, illiterate, ignorant in many ways, dull though he might be, in the council of the church found his voice and fulfilled a duty which would have tried the wisdom of the best educated and best instructed teacher.

Very soon the church began to realize itself. Sunday after Sunday the congregation sat discussing questions of church order, or instructing one another in the faith. Most often the missionary could not himself be present, and often when he might have been present, he felt that it was wise to leave his people to thresh out their questions and difficulties in their own way, and to report to him their decisions, or to send their questions to him, if they wanted his advice. He was not afraid that they would make serious mistakes or take hasty action behind his back. The more he retired from them, the more they turned to him in case of need, the more they sought his advice, the more they told him their plans, the more they saved him from difficulties. One day, on his return from an outlying village, he was met by his catechist with the familiar question: 'Do you know what we have been doing today?' 'No. What have you been doing?' 'We have adopted a baby.' The children of a poor Christian playing in the fields had heard a cry. Seeing no one near, they searched about till they discovered a box lightly covered with soil, from which the cry came. They broke it open and found a young baby. They took it home to their father. He, poor man, was utterly unable to satisfy another mouth. So next Sunday he went to church and told his tale. Thereupon the Christians decided to give it into the care of one of their number and to pay her a weekly dole for its maintenance. It was baptized with a name which in English means 'one who has obtained love'. When the missionary heard this he was glad. If he had not taught the people to 'Tell it to the church', the baby might have been put down on his doorstep, and he might have been driven to begin the foundation of a costly 'Foundlings' Home'. But happily for him, the church had learnt to manage its own business.

Sometimes it was his part to suggest the doing of charity. One day the catechist told him that the husband of a poor woman was dead, and the family was hard put to it to arrange the funeral. 'Get *so and so* to bring the case before the church.' After the meeting the missionary asked the catechist what the church had done. The church had subscribed *so much*. 'Is that enough?' 'Barely.' Then the missionary, too, as a member of the church, could subscribe. He was not outside the church. He could act with the church, but not instead of, or without it.

All this may sound very trivial. But yet it led the catechist to see the hope of a native church before him as a reality more clearly than all the teaching which he had received. And he learnt that lesson in three months. All the matters recorded here happened in less than six months, and he and many others had grasped the truth of the situation long before the end of that time. One day he came into the missionary's house with a question. 'Do you know what you are doing, sir?' 'Yes,' answered the missionary, 'I think that I know; but I should like to know what you think I am doing.' 'Well, sir, if you go on like this you will found a native church.'

Index to Bible References

Index of Bible References